AF755067

EMPOWERING RURAL WOMEN

EMPOWERING RURAL WOMEN

By

Dr. Minakshi
Dr. Sudarshan Mehta

ANMOL PUBLICATIONS PVT. LTD.
NEW DELHI - 110 002 (INDIA)

ANMOL PUBLICATIONS PVT. LTD.
4374/4B, Ansari Road, Daryaganj
New Delhi - 110 002
Ph.: 23261597, 23278000
Visit us at: www.anmolpublications.com

Empowering Rural Women
© Author

First Published, 2006

ISBN 81-261-2605-1

[All rights reserved. No part of this publication may be reproduced, stored in a retrieval system or transmitted, in any form or by any means, mechanical, photocopying, recording or otherwise, without prior written permission of the publisher.]

PRINTED IN INDIA

Published by J.L. Kumar for Anmol Publications Pvt. Ltd., New Delhi - 110 002 and Printed at Mehra Offset Press, Delhi.

CONTENTS

ACKNOWLEDGEMENTS

It is an immense feeling of pleasure to place on record my profound appreciation and deep sense of gratitude to my major advisor Dr. (Mrs.) Sudarshan Mehta, Associate Professor, Department of Home Science Extension Education, CCS Haryana Agricultural University, Hisar for her fruitful guidance and unfailing support during the course of study. I gratefully acknowledge her resolute guidance, unwavering encouragement, abiding interest, moral support and unparalleled care during this investigation.

I esteem it a privilege to express my deep sense of gratefulness to Dr. (Mrs.) N. Sethi, Professor (Home Science Extension Education); Dr. (Mrs.) S. Vermani, Professor (Sociology); Dr. Arjun Singh, Professor (Agricultural Economics); Dr. A.K. Gupta, Professor (Horticulture) and Dr. (Mrs.) N. Pruthi, Professor (Clothing and Textile) members of my advisory committee for their scholarly suggestions, constant help throughout the pursuit of this study and scrupulous editing of the manuscript.

I also owe my sincere gratefulness to Dr. (Mrs) Shashi K. Varma, Professor and Head, Department of Home Science Extension Education, for her cordial help and providing necessary facilities whenever necessary.

I take this opportunity to extend my sincere thanks to Dr. S.S. Jakhar, Department of Seed Science and Technology, and his family for the timely help, valuable guidance, cooperation and encouragement and providing homely atmosphere during this investigation.

I will be failing in my endeavours if I do not express my

sincere gratitude and warm regards to my parents-in-law for their day-today sacrifices and ready for help during the odd hours also. Sincere thanks are due to my sister-in-law, Mrs. Kanta Kundu and brother-in-law Sh. Aman Kundu. Words are short in expressing my sentiments towards my younger brother-in-law 'Kuku' for his graceful and affectionate inspiration and care which made it possible to complete this study in time. I am grateful to my husband Mr. Ravinder Kundu for his endless patience and facing the hard time with a lot of courage during this period. Likewise I am also thankful to my little kids 'Abhi Kundu' and 'Ishika' for their immense patience without my care during the course of current studies. I owe debt of gratitude to my beloved parents, brother Rohit and sister Ashima whose generous sacrifices, blessings, moral encouragements and good wishes have guided my efforts.

I shall always cherish the sweet memories and lively company and cooperation of all the friends. Heartily thanks also goes to Mr. Subhash Chander for meticulous word processing of the MSS.

Financial help provided by CCS Haryana Agricultural University as merit scholarship is duly acknowledged.

Last but not least we admire the Almighty Shiva as whole work is possible because of a unknown force which stood behind us as a strong pillar and provided us great zeal and enthusiasm by unknown sound, but known words to fulfil the dreams of that unknown, unseen, unborn face.

—MINAKSHI

LIST OF TABLES

1

INTRODUCTION

In olden days, flowers were not of much economic importance. One would grow flowers to fulfill his/her aesthetic sense. With the passage of time, there has been great change in life-style of people leading to commercialization of flowers growing. Today floriculture is recognized as a lucrative business since it has higher potential per unit area than most of the field crops even horticultural crops both for domestic market and export (Mishra & Pathania, 2000). The floriculture industry has a bright future as the global floriculture trade is growing at a very fast pace in the recent years. The world floriculture market is growing at an annual growth potential of 25-30 per cent foreign exchange earning ability than cereals.

With the implementation of World Trade Organization (WTO) provisions, the floriculture has received an impetus in recent years and it is emerging as major enterprise in world trade. Globally, trade of floriculture products is estimated to be US$ 52.24 million of which flowers and plants accounts for more than 80 per cent of total trade (Umrao & Singh, 1997).

More than 140 countries are now involved in floriculture. The share of developed countries is about 91 per cent where as developing countries contributes only 9 per cent in world trade of ornamentals. Inspite of having diverse soil, suitable agroclimatic conditions, large and reputed tissue culture facilities, expert and cheap manpower and developed industrial base, yet Indian share in world floriculture trade is less than one per cent. It is because, serious attention was not paid in the past to develop trade on scientific line to exploit its full potentialities.

Efforts on promoting commercial floriculture have started due to liberalization of industry and trade policies. Government of India has identified floriculture as an 'Extreme Focus Segment Item' during the Eighth Five-year Plan and has allocated an amount of Rs. 100 million for its development. It is taking various steps to remove some of the constraints and assist this sector to participate in floriculture export (Sindhu, 1995). Total export of floriculture during 2000-2001 was Rs. 105.49 crores. There is a vast scope for domestic market of around (estimated) Rs. 500 crores, in 2002. Delhi's market's share being about Rs. 50 crores annually (Mishra and Pathania, 2000). The total area under floriculture in India was 88,529 ha during 1999-2000 with production of 5,09,193 tonnes of loose flowers and 680.57 million of cut flowers. A beginning has been made recently. However, the flower production activities have been taken extensively only in few states till now. The major states being Karnataka, West Bengal, Tamil Nadu, Andhra Pradesh, Maharashtra, Utter Pradesh, Rajasthan, Haryana and Punjab having the largest area under flower production. Floriculture is popular in Haryana and cultivation of flowers is being taken up in the state on commercial lines and is turning more lucrative than other conventional agricultural crops. Haryana state have 2250 ha area with production of 40,500 tonnes of loose flowers and 76.00 millions cut flowers. It is very surprising that in 1962, there was only 4,000 ha land under flower cultivation which increased up to 88,527 ha in 2000 (ICAR, 2002).

In recent years, a few large business houses have entered

into floriculture for the production of cut flower for home consumption as also for export. However, the production and trade of floriculture for traditional and industrial purpose is mainly in hands of small family enterprises, where women folk is prominent worker, the poorer the family, the more it depends on economic productivity of its women. They have invisible hand, 90 per cent of rural women are unskilled and 88 per cent are illiterate which makes them vulnerable to exploit and economically dependent on men. No serious efforts have been made to improve the condition of women in our country. It is possible through empowerment of women. There is need to train women for the floriculture oriented enterpreneurship through which women of rural areas can easily earn money in short run by this occupation. Till now no training is given on floriculture even to men folk then what will be place of women. If women would be trained for the job related to flower cultivation, future prospect of floriculture would be brighter and so will be national development.

Keeping in view the increasing demand and better returns from flowers than agricultural crops, Haryana state Government has started taking steps to popularize commercial cultivation of flowers in 1993 to earn foreign currency. Sonepat is leading district in Haryana state which have large area under flower cultivation and in Panipat district, there is much potential for flower production. Both districts have proximity to national capital market of flowers. The present study is a pioneer attempt in this direction with the following objectives:

1. To study the existing pattern of flower cultivation technology
2. To impart technical know-how to rural women on flower cultivation

3. To analyze the acceptability level of flower cultivation enterprise by farm women.

Scope of Study

1. The study intends to explore acceptability and factors affecting adoption and non-adoption of floriculture among the rural women as an income generating activity. Based on this information, training approach for rural women development in diversified agriculture under similar agro-climatical conditions can be planned effectively.
2. The study is an attempt in the direction of highlighting the comprehensive information regarding existing knowledge, attitude, mental readiness to adopt, implementation and final adoption of flower cultivation by rural women and related constraints. Such information may be very useful for planning future course of action enabling various extension personnel in introducing other related innovation to rural women.
3. The technical material prepared under the study can be used for future by farm women farmers, field functionaries and other concerned directly or indirectly with flower cultivation.
4. Through present action research, flower cultivation has been proved to be profitable enterprise. This economic profitable aspect of flower cultivation will help other farm women in taking rational decision on the selection of this enterprise to be undertaken on their own farm.
5. The scope of study is not limited to Sonepat and Panipat districts but its findings could be used on similar conditions (socio-economic situations/area).

Limitation of the Study

1. The present study is being undertaken as a student research programme and hence it has limitations of resources particularly money and time.
2. Economically feasible flowers in Sonepat and Panipat districts may not be feasible in other districts, states or nations.
3. Initial investment is extremely high, beyond the reach of an average female working at farm.
4. Perishable nature of the crops, high investment, so greater risk factor.

2

REVIEW OF LITERATURE

A brief resume of past researches relevant to present study has been incorporated in this chapter.

2.1. Importance of Floriculture

Katyayan (1989) estimated that the volume of annual flower business in our country runs into 100 crores. The total area under cultivation extends to 20,600 hectares. Karnataka leads the nation in flower production. In an area of 6,900 hectares, 34,200 tons of flowers are produced in this state every year and this is about the one third of the national production. Among the flowers, almost 80% of flower trade is done in roses.

Behari (1993) reported that flowers can be used for decoration, adornment, garland making, banquets, extracting perfumes, preparation of Ayurvedic medicines, gulkand, essence industry, cosmetic preparation and soap manufacturing. Dried flowers, floral craft items and floral arrangement are used during festivals and marriages.

Pillay (1993) reported that quota restriction and complicated auction process are big hurdles, in addition to these, exporters have to pay heavily for obtaining flower varieties from foreign sources. They have to fight against land ceiling acts. The storage facilities for ready to export flowers and air transport services have to be improved.

National Horticulture Board (1995) reported that Board is providing assistance to the tune of 50 per cent under different heads as given: Grading / packing (Rs. 6,10,000), rental sale centres (Rs. 18,000), rental sale air conditioned centres (Rs. 75,000), specific transport vehicle (Rs. 1,70,000), cold transport vehicle (5,00,000), pre-cooling unit (Rs. 5,00,000), cold storage house (Rs. 35,00,000), sale point (Rs. 50,000), maturing & curing chamber (Rs. 50,000), plastic karret (subsidy) Rs 70/- or 50 per cent whichever is less.

In addition Board also provide assistance of soft loan for marketing and development of horticulture production for introduction of new technology & concept, training and visit plan for farmers, financial assistance to institutions involved in horticulture development.

Sandhu (1995) reported that Govt. is stressing on floriculture and identified floriculture as 'thrust area'. The Haryana Govt. has announced a subsidy ranging from Rs. 32,000 to Rs. one lakh per greenhouse of 500 sq. meters. He also emphasized that the Government of India has identified floriculture as an 'Extreme Focus Segment Item' during the Eighth five year plan. And allocated an amount of Rs. 100 million for the development of floriculture.

Srivastava (1995) analysed that the world trade of flowers is estimated at $25 billion. Netherland controlling about 60 per cent market, followed by Columbia (10%), Italy (6%) and Israel (4). Indian share in exports of flowers is negligible (0.06%). During 1992-93, India exported cut flowers worth Rs. 8.44 crores aggregate flower export of about Rs. 15 crores. The export target of floriculture products during 1994-95 i.e. Rs. 50 crores however expected to be achieved without difficulty. The top cut flowers traded in the world market are rose and chrysanthemum and demand for these flowers has been growing at a rate of 17 per cent for rose and seven per cent for chrysanthemum. The cost of production of flower in India is much cheaper compared to that of Europe, because in Europe they have to invest more on construction of green houses and pay more wages. The government of India has rightly declared floriculture as an important thrust area in 1992 and has targeted an export of Rs. 120 crores by 1996-97 and Rs. 200 crores by the turn of the century.

Acharyya and Panda (1996) emphasized that India's share in multi billion global floriculture market which has been growing by 15 to 17 per cent per annum, is less than one per cent. A survey pegged flower production in the country at 2.07 lakh tones of loose flowers and Rs. 45 crore pieces of cut flowers per annum. Exports from India accounted about Rs. 30.60 crore in 1994-95 and the eighth plan-working group has based the estimates on 30,924 hectares under floriculture.

Chhabra (1996) concluded that the international floriculture trade is estimated to be of the order of $ 40 billion and this is growing at a very fast of about 15 to 20 per cent. Cut flowers account for about 60 per cent of this turnover. However, India's share of $ 20 million worth of exports is just 0.5 per cent of the global trade and it is expected to increase to $ 43 million by 1997. Production of cuts flower is likely to reach a level of 20,000 tonnes by the year 2000.

For encouraging this industry government established country's first auction house in Bangalore in November 1995 and the first national conference on floriculture was also held in October 1995.

Reddy (1996) reported that India's share in the world market is negligible. Floriculture here still in its infancy but picking up fast. It has good potential for foreign earnings, if the Government initiates measures to grow flower on scientific lines as in Holland, the U.K. and the U.S., Japan and Thailand.

Sebastian (1996) emphasized that cultivating roses in one hectare needs an investment of about Rs. 6,000. The Govt. provides assistance to new farmers to the tune of Rs. 1,000 in the form of plants and chemicals. On an average one kg of fresh roses fetches Rs. 15. The dry petals of the flowers are a value-added product which fetch around Rs. 100 per kg. In case of dried buds of roses, which are much in demand abroad, the price is Rs. 300 per kg.

Ambad (1997) reported that the flowers are used for decorating homes by all classes of the people. They express beauty and extend the love. The flowers arranged after some pattern, may be relaxing and enjoyable hobby. Many people including professionals, florists, men and women and youngsters enjoy this art. Florists enjoy expressing their sentiments through flowers.

According to the then Agriculture Minister Chaturanan Mishra on March 18th ,1997, the Government is implementing a central Sector Scheme on commercial floriculture in all the states/ UT's of country at a total cost of Rs. 14.29 crores. The National Horticulture Board provides financial assistance in the form of soft loan for integrated projects on floriculture on project basis. In addition APEPA (Ministry of Commerce) has schemes for infrastructure development and market support for floriculture projects for export.

Chauhan (1997) observed that flowers not only have great importance in worship, decoration, garlanding and place beautification but also provide good economic returns to the growers. As per rough estimate the area under floriculture in the country was about 3,500 hectare during 1993-94. Among the flowers, cultivation of marigold is comparatively easy and its flowers can be kept for a longer time. Marigold cultivation is labour intensive, its cultivation is possible where there is plenty of labour which is abundant in India.

Jadhav *et.al.* (1997) pointed out that floriculture international market is growing at 10-15 per cent and domestic market at 25-30 per cent, there is an unlimited scope for expanding floriculture activity. The government of India has identified floriculture as 'extreme focus thrust area' for export. According to an estimate India will earned a foreign exchange of Rs. 200 crore by the end of this century.

Misra (1997) emphasized that Delhi is among the prominent flower centers in the country. Of the total flower trade of about Rs. 250 crore in the country, the capital's share is Rs. 30 crore.

Sindhu and Misra (1997) pointed out that Netherland is the biggest exporter (59%), followed by Columbia (10%) and Italy (6%). Recently Kenya and Israel have also started exporting the flowers, accounting one and four per cent respectively. The other countries including developing ones have only 20 per cent of the total export, India's share in the total world export being less than one per cent. The growth pattern of floriculture in India was 10 per cent in 1991-92 and 1992-93, 15 per cent in 1993-94 and 1994-95 & 1995-96 it was 20 per cent.

Singh (1997) emphasized that floriculture is a fast emerging industry in India, as it has increased 12.5 times in area and 33 times in trade from 1962 to 1991. This increase in area and trade is because of socio-economic factors such as changes in social values of people, environment, and increase in population and living standard. The growth of floriculture industry was very slow from 1962 go 1990. Then there has been a significant rise in floriculture export form Rs. 14.45 crores n 1991-92 to Rs. 30.60 crores in 1994-95 and Rs. 57.80 crores in 1995-96. Developing countries have only 6% share in world market. This help in increasing the export from India, which is otherwise negligible. The annual growth rate of domestic trade in floriculture products is estimated to be 15-20%.The major flower growing countries are Holland, Columbia, Italy, Israel, Germany and Mexico. The leading flower growing states in India are Karnataka, Andhra Pradesh, Tamil Nadu, West Bengal, Maharashtra and Utter Pradesh.

Umrao *et.al.* (1997) reported that more than 140 countries are now involved in floriculture. The share of developed countries is about 91 per cent where as developing countries contributes only 9 per cent in world trade of ornamentals. Inspite of having diverse soil, agroclimatic and geographical area yet Indian share in world floriculture trade is less than one per cent.The world floriculture market is growing at an annual growth potential of 25-30 per cent foreign exchange earning ability.

Apte and Bhargava (1998) found that with the implementation of eighth five year plan (1992-97) in India, Government allocated an amount of Rs. 1,000 crores for the horticulture sector as against Rs. 24 crores in seventh plan, an unprecedented boost to the floriculture. Result of this investment was that India has indeed made an entry in the world floriculture trade, however insignificant (share of 1% or less). The export value of cut flowers increased three times.

Mishra (1998) emphasised that Delhi is among he prominent flower centers in the country.Of the total flower trade of about Rs. 250 crore in the country, the capital's share is Rs. 30 crore.

Ghosh (1999) estimated on the basis of available information that about 70,000 ha is covered under flowers based on the information available for cut flowers use. Another about 500 ha of climatically controlled green houses is reported to be available for growing quality flowers for export. As per

APEDA source, during 1997-98, India's export earnings from floriculture was Rs. 775 million. It is estimated that annual growth rate of domestic trade of floriculture products is about 25-30 per cent.

Choudhary and Prasad (2000) drawn conclusion that India's share in global floriculture trade is almost minuscule (0.4% of total value), however, this nascent industry registered as phenomenal growth from a mere 14.91 crores in 1992-93 to 80.00 crores by the end of 1998-99. Indian floriculture industry has gone through 2 distinct phases. The first phase (1991-97) was a learning phase where the dependency was more on importing technology, machinery, auction marketing and buy-back system. The second phase (1997-99 onwards) is characterized by fine tuning the technology to Indian needs, venturing into direct marketing, good export growth, more price realization, stabilizing production and marketing relationship.

Rao (2000) reported that floriculture has been identified as an 'extreme focus area' for special attention of the government, for thrust in exports and rightly so this is an area with abundant potential which has unfortunately remained untapped till now.

Raghava (2001) analyzed that in 1998-99, the export of valuable floriculture products was Rs. 99.05 crores, showing a remarkable growth in the sector. India occupied fifteenth position in the flower exports to European Union markets during 1995. The diversification in floricultural products is a viable and economically- sustainable to the growers in India. (The world floriculture product trade has reached $ 50 billion mark). Besides this National Horticulture Board is providing soft loans to various entrepreneurs at very nominal interest. NABARD is also giving loans for growing flowers for domestic and international markets. Many 'Model Floriculture Centers' have been established in different states for the development of this industry in India. The flowers growing have been practiced in India for religious, aesthetic values, social functions, besides extraction of essential oils and manufacturing perfumes. Now flowers are also being grown for their use in banquets and interior decorations. Besides, India is endowed with diverse agroclimatic conditions, which provide ample opportunities for the productions of all major flowers throughout the year in one part or the other.

Raj (2001) analyzed that export potential of cut flower was 1003.30 lakhs, dried flower was 3,645.56 lakhs and bulks of Rs. 192.16 lakhs out of total floricultural products (6014.15 lakhs) from India during 1995-96. The floral crafts are sold at the rate of Rs. 50-200/piece in domestic markets whereas in Europe, USA and Japan 10-15 time higher returns was earned. It is more profitable and lucrative business.

Saini (2001) reported that major varieties of gladiolus cultivated for commercial purpose are : Snow Princess, Friendship, Oscar, Yellow Stone, Rose Supreme, Mayur.

The Agricultural Processed Food Export Development Authority (APEDA) has estimated 34,000 hectares under flower production which include 24,000 hectares under traditional and 10,000 hectares under exotic flowers. The return estimated is around Rs. 205 crores comprising of Rs. 105 crores of traditional flower business and Rs. 100 crores for the exotic flower trade whereas the international floriculture market trade is estimated to be 40 billion US dollars (Rs. 1,25,000 crore) of which cut flowers account for nearly 60 per cent i.e. 25 billion US dollars (Rs. 80,000 crores). The latest estimates of annual global flower trade is worth 2,500 million US dollars and the Indian contribution at present is about 0.36 million US dollars.

Chaudhary and Prasad (2002) emphasized that the global floriculture trade is expanding at the rate of 15 per cent / annum, whereas in India the annual growth is around 7-8 per cent. Interestingly, the domestic market that was predominantly ruled by the loose traditional flowers started absorbing cut flowers i.e. in Bangalore alone, the local auctions rose from Rs. 3 lakh in 1996-97 to Rs. 4.00 crores in 1999-2000.

Dadlani (2002) observed that with more than 80,000 ha, India is leading country for floriculture in terms of area while our exports of floricultural products worth less than 3 crores US dollars. The total value of exports has jumped from about Rs. 14 crores in 1991-92 to more than Rs. 200 crores in 2000-2001. Nearly two–third of this trade is actually the dried flowers and plants. The cut flower export from less than Rs. 40 lakh worth of our exports in 1991-92, the value has risen to nearly Rs. 40 crores in 2000-2001. More than 90% of the exporters grow rose. Rose continues to be ranked number one in the export trade and command a premium price.

Mishra and Dhankar (2002) reported that the export of floricultural products has increased from Rs. 8.00 crores (1990-91) to Rs. 87.00 crores (1997-98). During 2000-2001, the export of floriculture has gone up to Rs. 123.12 crores. Out of total exports, dried flowers account for more than 60 per cent and normally 80 per cent of the total dried flowers are the collection from the wild.

Parameswaran (2002) reported that flowers in the form of garland are used on auspicious occasions like marriage and temple rites. They are part of life and also used in therapy. Flowers are used as the foundation for making various kinds of medicines. It can be used for therapy in the form of seeing i.e. 'darsanam', wearing and smelling etc. 'Pushpa Ayurveda' seems to have got a new lease of life. Several reputed ayurveda institutions in the private sector have come forward.

Sharma (2002) attempted to analyze that National Bank for Agriculture and Rural Development (NABARD) promotes floricultural crops by loan to growers. Floriculture as on today is occupying a total area of 73,970.88 ha in the country. The total refinance so far been given to floriculture industry from 1992-93 to 2000-2001 is to the tune of Rs. 9,556.382 lakhs during 2000-2001 an amount of Rs. 1,555 lakhs has been disbursed which contributes 6.3 per cent of total refinance of horticulture and plantation crops.

Singh (2002) examined that consumption of flowers has increased manifold. The total world export of floricultural products in 2000 was of US $ 7,662,924,000. The Netherland remained world's largest exporter of floricultural products. With a share of almost 50 per cent of the total exports, India rank 22nd with export of 26,971,000 US $. Germany was the largest importing country. It imported floricultural products worth US $ 1,457,696,000. Consumption of cut flowers in Western Europe was 11 billion US $ in 1990 and 14 billion US $ 1995 which reached to 20 billion US$ in 2001.

In India, the flowers are grown all over the country in 88,607 ha and the production of flowers is estimated to be more than 5 lakh tones of loose flowers and over 680 million cut flowers. In Haryana area under flower cultivation was 2250 hectare while 40,500 tonnes loose flower and 760 lakh cut flowers in 1999-2000. The flowers are generally purchased for gift (45%), special occasions such as birthday and wedding (25%) and for home decoration.

Singh *et.al.*, (2002) reported that cut flowers are grown in 86,000 ha with a production of 5,09,200 tonnes of loose flower and 680.60 million in number (1999-2000).

2.2. Women Participation and Exposure to Flower Cultivation

Pradhan (1990) told that the women contribute in different ways to agriculture in different states of India. They function as nursery growers, fish sellers, fruit and vegetables vendors, labour for transplanting of seeds, spinning of the wool, weaving of pankhi. No serious efforts have been made to improve the condition of women in our country.

If women would be trained for these jobs, future prospect of agricultural sector would be brighter. After training, helps should be provided so that woman establishes their self-employment programmes.

Sen and Rani (1990) discussed that the incidence of women's participation in the labour force and their contribution to the total family income are higher in households with lower economic status. The poorest families are most dependent upon women's economic productivity. About 35 per cent of Indian households below the poverty line are headed by women and thus, in most case dependent exclusively on female income.

Kaptan (1994) revealed that there are more than 1,53,260 women entrepreneurs, 9.1 per cent of total 1.70 million entrepreneurs in India. Of these majority are in low paid, low skilled, low technology and low production jobs in industries, handicraft, handlooms and cottage industries. Considering the trend, women's participation in industries is likely to scale up to 20 per cent, thus raising the number of women entrepreneurs to about 5,00,000. A large number of women entrepreneurs in rural areas are likely to be developed for small business.

Mishra (1994) estimated that 94 per cent of the women workers are engaged in the unorganized sectors of the economy and among the women employed in unorganized sector, 80.1

per cent and 19.9 per cent are respectively employed in agriculture and non- agricultural occupations. As per 1991 census, 46.18 per cent of the total women workers are agricultural worker.

Rao (1994) examined that 85 per cent of those involved in dairying activities in India are women. Women handle most of the productive aspects of animal care.

Uberoy (1995) reported that in India, agriculture accounts for 32 per cent of the net national product. Among 70 per cent of the total working population, 84 per cent of all economically active women are involved in agriculture. Women make up 46 per cent of the agriculture work force. Statistical data showed that there was a progressive increase in the number of women involved both as cultivators and wage workers. But a scrutiny of the situation behind the statistical figures indicates that women were vital and productive workers. The poorer the family, the more it depends on the economic productivity of its women.

Widge (1995) observed that the male cultivators have increased in the country by 11.67 per cent from 7.67 crore in 1981 to 8.56 crore in 1991. The female cultivators, however, increased at a much faster rate of 45.23 per cent from 1.48 crores in 1981 to 2.15 crores in 1991. The number of male agricultural labourers increased by 31.18 per cent from 3.47 crore in 1981 to 4.55 crore in 1991. Female agricultural labourers increased by a slightly higher percentage of 36.15 from 2.08 crore in 1981 to 2.82 crore in 1991.

Rai (1996) reported that agriculture continues to be the mainstay of the women's employment in India. Nearly 78 per cent of the economically active female population in the country is engaged in agriculture as compared to nearly 63 per cent of men. Almost 50 per cent of the rural female worker are classified as agriculture labourers and 37 per cent as cultivators.

Studies from other countries showed that if women farmers had the same inputs as men, output could be raised by 10-20 per cent.

Khader (1997) reported that 40 women respondents among mushrooms growers were selected for training organized at college of Home Science, Bhapatla for investigation and found that rural women can easily manage 4-10 beds depending upon the space available.

Latha and Brindha (1997) concluded that women in hybrid seed production are preferred, as the job is meticulous, need patient and delicate handling. The farm owner values female skilled labour and they do not want to lose them at any cost. Skilled women are able to command higher wages and have bargaining power with their employer. The employers try to retain the skilled female labour by providing them advance money.

Islam (1998) analysed women's participation in agricultural income generating activities. The findings indicated that age and family size of participating women had no significant relationships with their extent of participation but education, mass media exposure, contact with extension agents, and their husband's attitude were found to be significantly associated with women's extent of participation in income generating activities.

Sharma (1999) found that the proportionate contribution of women in mushroom cultivation was found to be higher than men.

Qaim (1999) noted that self help group were more successful than the Government-induced groups, however, proved to be the women's own grassroots initiations.

Anita (2000) concluded that among the adopters of mushrooms production technology, 22.50 per cent respondents put it into practice immediately after training while 6.25 per cent respondents tried the technology after some persuasion (2-3 visits).

Bala (2000) reported that in Moga district of Punjab, participation of farm women was higher in uprooting of seedlings, transplanting as regards pre-harvest agricultural activities. Women participation was more in nursery raising, hoeing and weeding operations.

Chattopadhyay (2000) drawn inferences that due to intensive and specialized type of work, floriculture enterprise engages 8-10 skilled and unskilled workers per hectare throughout the year in addition to a large number of self employed workers for processing, transportation and marketing. At present 1.73 million of workers are engaged in various operations of the enterprise in the state starting from the production to ultimate sale to the consumers which makes an approximate turnover of Rs. 79.0 crores of rupees annually.

Gill (2002) reported that participation of farm women in pre-sowing and post sowing and harvesting activities in terms of decision making was found to be low with overall mean score 0.28,0.24 and 0.50 respectively.

2.3. Assessing the Acceptability of Floriculture Technology

2.3.1. *Knowledge Gain*

Anita (2000) revealed that the respondents gained high level of knowledge in loaning/expected income (76.25%) fruiting/harvesting (56.25%), packing/marketing (56.25%), and casing (51.25%) in order of sequence. This was followed by medium knowledge gain in spawn /spawning/ filling (53.75%), food value (48.75%), composting (46.25%), concept/ importance (46.25%) and precautions/limitations (38.75%), whereas 60 per cent respondents gained low knowledge in kinds of mushroom. The training on mushroom technology helped the respondents to gain knowledge.

Mehta (1995) found that there was significant reduced knowledge gap in all the mushroom cultivation messages at post-exposure stages due to training. In addition to this, trainees having lower level of initial knowledge had higher scope of improvement in the knowledge through training.

Sangwan (2002) analysed that majority of rural women had high knowledge level and developed favourable attitude after receiving training on grape products.

2.3.2. *Attitude Change*

Mehta (1995) inferred that training proved effective in creating favourableness towards mushroom cultivation technology.

Anita (2000) calculated that a large number of respondents (63.75%) had favorable (50.00%) and strongly favorable (13.75%) followed by unfavorable (36.25%) attitude towards mushroom production technology at pre-exposure stage. But after training majority (76.25%) of the respondents had their swing towards strongly favorable (38.75%) and favorable (37.50%) attitude towards this technology. Only 23.75 per cent respondents were having unfavorable attitude.

2.3.3. *Decision (Adoption Feasibility/Symbolic Adoption)*

Latha and Brindha (1994) revealed that women are consulted at each and every step of seed production. They decide which company to work with. They also choose the seeds to be produced and allocate the land area for seed production.

Mehta (1995) emphasised that there occurred definite shift in the level of symbolic adoption on account of training indicating thereby that training can bring change in symbolic adoption.

Patel *et al.* (1996) indicated that majority (71%) of rural women alone made decision on storage of grains for home consumption and other purposes. On the other hand decision on animal husbandry activities, expenditure pattern, education and marriage of children were made by men & women jointly. It was also observed that decision on cropping pattern and marketing of the produce was made by men folk alone in majority of the cases.

Dahiya (1999) concluded that majority of the respondents (67%) had low level of adoption of floriculture followed by medium (23%) and high (10%). Further she had also concluded that majority of the farmers having medium and high level of adoption were Saini, below 45 years, literate, belonged to nuclear families, having medium level of family literacy index. These respondents were having more than Rs. 15,000 per capita income. Farmers having frequent contacts with Horticultural Development Officers and District Extension Specialist had high level of adoption. Majorities of the respondents having no contacts with private dealers were medium adopters'. Majority of the farmers had medium level of economic motivation and scientific orientation, were medium and high adopters of floriculture.

Anita (2000) stated that out of total sample adoption feasibility was high of 65.00 per cent respondents followed by 32.50 per cent respondents having medium adoption feasibility of mushroom production technology.

Nearly half of the respondents (48.75%) were found to be more confident in accepting mushroom cultivation due to know-how received through training followed by 45.00 per cent respondents fully convinced about the importance of mushroom cultivation and were of the opinion that no one can stop them to implement it. Almost similar percentage of respondents (43.75%) who found it an easy technology inspite of requiring certain precautions.

2.3.4. *Implementation/Confirmation (Adoption)*

Anita (2000) observed that among the adopters 22.50 per cent respondents put mushroom production technology into practice immediately after training while 6.25 per cent respondents tried the technology after some persuation (2-3 visits).

Sangwan (2002) reported that most of rural women had low adoption feasibility level before the training, while half of the respondents had high adoption feasibility level after the training.

Confirmation

Reddy (1996) compared India with Japan and said in Japan at place Jamaica, 100 growers set up their floriculture farm of 1,000 square meter size. The Jamaican Govt. set up a marketing company which gives inputs to the farmers, picks up the produce and market it, thereby saving the farmers cost of marketing and transport. These 100 growers had adopted floriculture as success. Perhaps India could learn a lesson or two from Jamaican, as majority of its farmers are small and marginal category.

Anita (2000) revealed that total 53.75 per cent respondents adopted the technology out of which 43.75 per cent respondents adopted immediately after completion of first crop of mushroom, whereas 10 per cent cultivated after some persuasion (one visit).

Overall Acceptability

Das and Mitra (1994) concluded that after seeing cost return analysis data per acre has motivated traditional farmers, particularly small and marginal to grow this crop (marigold) extensively in the flower growing regions.

2.4. Constraints Related to Floriculture

Padmanabhan (1991) concluded in eight plan Working Group Report, the constraints to development of floriculture include: lack of scientific information, inadequate extension services to ensure transfer of research results to the growers, inadequacy of trained personnel, non-availability of quality seeds and planting material in large quantities, lack of infra structural facilities such as cold rooms to cool the cut flowers, air conditioned trucks for transport, packaging materials, non availability of green house materials etc.

Pillay (1993) drawn conclusion that there are some factors which favours this industry are : suitable agro-climatic conditions, large and reputed tissue culture facilities. Best of all, it has expert, cheap man power availability and developed industrial base is an added asset.However the quota restriction and complicated auction process are big hurdles, in addition to these exporters have to pay heavily for obtaining flower varieties from foreign sources. They have to fight against land ceiling acts. The storage facilities for ready to export flowers and air transport service have to be improved.

Ramphal (1993) reported that there are several constraints in national and international trade of flower and these are: generally low yield and high cost of production, no direct air links between local production centers and foreign procuring centers, facilities of cold store chain from production center to airport are not available, high air freight and limited/ inadequate air cargo space, export feasibility studies are not available adequately, absence of organized marketing channels and monitoring systems, heavy duty on imports increases the cost of floricultural inputs, several procedural bottlenecks & existing law discourage exports and modern floriculture is a highly capital intensive industry.

Sharma (1993) found some of the most important factors to be considered during post-harvest handling of flowers are : initial quality, pests and diseases, rapid handling, cooling, water supply and loss, physical and ethylene damage and packaging.

Das and Mitra (1994) analysed that major constraints faced by the cultivators of marigold are fluctuation of prices, lack of perfect knowledge of market- prices forces the actual cultivators to receive less than what ought to be.

Sindhu (1995) reported that several constraints in export of cut flower, floricultural products at production, transport and marketing levels. Some of these are : capital intensive industry, require technologically advanced infra structure, lack of quantity of good material, lack of technical experts, absence of cold chain from production site to airport, poor packing of cut flowers, inadequate incentives to the farmers, financial support and unorganized marketing channels and their monitoring, insufficient cold storage at airport, low priority in air Cargo as they are bulky, voluminous and perishable. The agro based industry so susceptible to vagaries of weather, pest etc., land ceiling act, gestation period of Industry is very long and therefore, over dependence on foreign collaborators are the constraints in the growth of floriculture industry. Moreover the domestic market of flowers is very poor therefore, increases international marketing risk too. The reasons or factors responsible for slow flower market in India are : demand and supply of flower in the Indian market is highly seasonal, volume of flowers coming to the market varies significantly on day to day basis, seasonal availability of specific flower, significant variation in prices of flowers on day to day and with in a day basis, domestic demands are highly uncertain, consumer preference of floriculture products are not only different in different market but change rapidly.

Vasavada (1995) found some favourable factors for the flower cultivation in India are diverse agro-climatic and ecological conditions, infrastructure including communication, roads, international airports are developed, very skilled and cost effective manpower as well as labour force is available in country, greenhouse facilities are available at much lower costs. Some unfavorable factors in which one is seed policy, which did not permit easy import of planting material, as long as suitable planting material is not available, it is simply not possible to grow and market the floricultural products accepted in world markets. Similarly, regulations regarding quarantine at the time of import, facilities and procedures to be followed at the time of export and such factors are so cumbersome and impractical that it was not possible to effectively handle perishable floricultural products.

Acharyya and Panda(1996) and also Singh(1994) reported that India's poor performance in the global flower market is due to its inadequate infra structure for the production of floral crops for export, lack of appropriate planting materials, production technology, basic inputs like standard containers, quality packing materials are critical bottlenecks. Suitable market surveys and pricing informations are not available. Sales promotion activities are meager. Also there is lack of quality control mechanism and coordination between government and floriculture firms. Absence of cold chains, exorbitant freight charges around $ 3 per kg, ex-India is a daunting problem. Domestic market is unorganized and there is no established marketing channels.

Chhabra (1996) concluded factors that leads this industry at slow rate are : European community imposes a 10 per cent import duty on flower imports from India, while imports from Africa and Israel do not have any duty. The Dutch impose 20 per cent duty on Indian exports. Exports have to pay Rs. 80 per kg as freight cost, import duty of Rs. 15 per kg in on-season and Rs. 20 per kg in off-season, besides 10-12 per cent as auction house charges and commission to agents.

Kundu *et.al.*(1997) reported that India's poor performance in global market is because of inadequate infra structure, lack of appropriate planting materials, production technology, basic inputs like standard containers, quality packing materials etc. are critical bottlenecks. Suitable market surveys and pricing information are not available. Absence of control mechanism and coordination between government and flori-firms. Absence of cold chains, exorbitant freight charges, and domestic market is unorganized and there is no established marketing channel.

Maity (1997) found that main constraints in flower cultivation are technical in nature i.e. dissemination of knowledge to flower growers through training has yet remained in the rudimentary stage. There are transport problems like export oriented floricultural units located at a distance, unassured availability of cargo space in the plane, tax is often levied on export consignment of flowers by both the exporting and importing countries and marketing problem i.e. unsold flowers are often lost.

Apte and Bhargava (1998) concluded that major obstacles in export of cut flowers are : poor quality produce, unorganized industry, high air freight costs, import duties in the European Union, a total lack of research, teaching, training and extension education facilities.

Training for even the personnel engaged in floriculture units is not available either in any of the agricultural universities or at any other organization in India.

Dahiya (1999) concluded that under cultivation constraints majority of the respondents faced lack of awareness about large number of varieties for commercial cultivation, labour intensive profession and fear of natural hazards. Regarding storage constraints, lack of standard containers followed by damage of flowers due to lack of storage facilities. Whereas, ten per cent exorbitant commission from the farmers, wide fluctuation in prices, monopoly of private commission agents in fixing prices and no support price by the government were the marketing constraint being faced by the farmers.

Gosh (1999) found that major constraints related to technology are: small and unirrigated land holdings, large tracks of low and unproductive plantations need replacement, low productivity of crops due to inferior genetic stocks and poor management, inadequate supply of quality planting materials of improved varieties, high incidence of pests and diseases, heavy post-harvest losses and low utilization in the processing sector, poor infrastructure and absence of market information system.

Talukdar and Karmakar (1999) identified the problem faced in decision making in agriculture. The major problems faced were lack of economic resources under their command (90%), lack of pertinent facts or knowledge about agriculture (81%) and lack of contact with information sources (87%). The other important problems faced were lack of support from extension agencies, lack of command in implementation, low educational status and low mobility.

Chattopadhyay (2000) found that lack of commercial outlook of industrial houses, bad surface communication system, limitation of land ceiling, lack of storage facilities & cold chain in airport, non-cooperation of financial institutions, Govt. encouragement is not appreciable, lack of auction market, direct and regular air services to international floriculture market and cost of air service is high.

Raut and Rasane (2000) concluded that the requirement of more labour for grading and packing, high cost of packing material, high transport cost, absence of open auction method of sale, low price and the high commission in Mumbai market were the important constraints in marketing of rose flowers as reported by farmers.

Anita (2002) reported that non-availability of compost in time, poor quality compost and low per cent germination of spawn are main input constraint. Training not sufficient, lack of technical know-how are the technical constraints and lack of complete knowledge about government help in the form of credit and subsidy (100%), not able to follow complicated procedure for obtaining loan from financial institution (100%), lack of complete knowledge about precautionary issues involved (45.65%), lack of knowledge regarding optimum temperature (91.30%) and lack of complete knowledge about different stages of mushroom production (52.17%), lack of financial assistance was reported by majority of (73.91%) respondents as main economic constraint.

Dhawan (2002) reported that in India, we have over 34,000 ha of area under flower cultivation. We do not figure anywhere in the world trade. Importing planting material at a very high price, varieties which were not sold at premium price, high interest rate on the infrastructure, cost and high energy costs for running greenhouses are the reasons for dismal performance of this industry.

Misra and Dhankar (2002) concluded that cold storage facilities, transportation facilities, unorganized market, middlemen and commission agents swallow the major share and hardly 30-40 per cent of money reaches the real grower, mob mentality, lack of technical know-how, inclement weather, improper sanitation of the field and indiscriminate use of pesticides are the major hindrances in flower growing.

Negi (2002) highlighted some marketing bottlenecks, these are : About 75 per cent of the farmers sell their produce at the farm level to village merchants, retailers, contractors so low price obtained, non availability of transportation, malpractices in market such as heavy deduction, free sample of the produce, high and unjust market charges, delayed payments, pooling by traders and lack of open bid system.

Small unorganized farmers and lack group action and bargaining power. There is no organized concessional credit available to the farmers. Information regarding demand, supply, price, market out look knowledge of consumers, preference, marketing channels and practices are important for marketing of produce, which is not available at the moment. The small and marginal farmers are not attended properly by the commission agents. These farmers have to wait for a long period for auction of their produce.

Sharma (2002) reported that indigenous varieties of plants, production and post- harvest technologies are not adequately developed to meet the international quality standards, lack of market information and expertise and so dependence on foreign marketing agencies, lack of cold storage facilities at airports, inadequacy of air cargo space, delay in clearance of import of exotic plants and seed materials are constraints in financing floriculture projects.

Singh (2002) found that availability of quality planting material, traditional flower oriented technology, infrastructure and marketing, package of practices for traditional and modern cut flowers under different agro climatic conditions are major constraints in development of floriculture industry.

2.5. Factors Affecting Adoption and Non-Adoption

Anita (2000) concluded that the main reasons for non-adoption of mushroom technology were shortage of space in home, lack of time, highly perishable crop and less mutual cooperation among women for composting.

Sharma (2003) found that education was found to be

positively correlated with knowledge and attitude but negatively correlated with symbolic adoption as highly educated people showed least interest towards performance of agricultural operations.

Anita (2000) concluded that the economic motivation emanated as the main contributory factor to change attitude decision to adopt, implement, confirm and accept the mushroom cultivation technology.

Sangwan (2002) reported that risk orientation and land holding of grape growing women were found to be significantly associated with knowledge and attitude.

Sharma (2003) illustrated that respondent with higher communication & situational variables had higher overall knowledge and attitude but their symbolic adoption was negatively associated with these variables.

2.6. Economic Feasibility of Floriculture

Gaikwad (1981) showed that in chrysanthemum crop out of gross returns of Rs. 8,699.22 per acre, the total cost of production was Rs. 4,072.75 in which the major item of expenditure was that of marketing.

Das and Mitra (1994) analyzed that cost of production of marigold is Rs. 5,522 per acre. Leaving the inputs of family labour component, its cost cultivation comes to Rs. 3,827 per acre while farm business income is as high as Rs. 11,923.23. This figure is too lucrative in comparison to other comparative traditional crops. This crop has other plus point that it has its nil expenditure in the component of fixed cost.

Kadian *et.al.* (1995) quoted that National Commission on Agriculture has target of 5,00,000 hectares flower cultivation area by the year 2000AD. Among the flowers, gladiolus is the highest paying crop as it fetches net return of Rs. 59,679 per acre while the rose gives. Rs. 7,107 and marigold gives Rs. 1091 per acre respectively.

Kundu (1997) made inferences that floriculture industry export is growing at a compound growth rate of about 4 per cent (3.89), which indicates credible performance of India's floricultural export, project's.

Dahiya *et.al.*(1999) reported that under present production technology and relative price structure, the flower crops i.e. marigold and gladiolus were found to be considerable more profitable in comparison to their competing crops. The return over variable cost and total cost per hectare of marigold was relatively higher (Rs. 32,823 and 20,295) then its competing crops paddy (Rs. 18,980 and 9,827) and arhar (Rs. 9000 and Rs. 3,380). In case of gladiolus, the return over variable cost (Rs. 1,38,418) and total cost (Rs. 78,808) was substantially higher as compared to its competing crops i.e. mustard (Rs. 10,418 and Rs. 358) and wheat (9,937 and 1,372).

Goyal (1999) found that the reasonable rate of return could be taken up to 10 years of age from rose crop. The yield per hectare was estimated to be 23 quintals in first year of establishment. The yield increased up to 67 quintals per hectare in third year.

Singh and Bijimol (1999) analysed that growing gladiolus is lucrative as, after cultivation of gladiolus on one hectare he found that net profit of Rs. 5,28,978.00 can be obtained after investing Rs. 8,56,022.

Anita (2000) calculated that total production cost of mushroom cultivation was reported as Rs. 2,125, which include expenses on raw material and manpower both. Gross return was found to be Rs. 10,000. Net return came to be Rs. 7,875. Analysis further reflected that total cost per kg was found to be Rs. 10.62 and net return per respondent was observed as Rs. 342.39.

Dahiya and Goyal (2000) found that rose cultivation in Sonepat district is economically viable and cost effective based on its economic analysis i.e. benefit-cost ratio (8.48), Average annual net return Rs. 444.57 and pay back period (1.10 years).

De and Dhiman (2001) calculated that a farmer can earn Rs. 30,000/ha/year from rose after investing Rs. 1,00,000 for cultivating rose for 5 years, from gladiolus can earn Rs. 1,00,000-2,50,000/ha, from tuberose can earn Rs. 60,000-1,00,000/ha, from marigold farmer can earn Rs. 50,000-1,00,000/ha and from chrysanthemum grower can earn Rs. 1.5-2 lakh/ha/year.

Tomar and Singh (2001) revealed that expenditure of marigold crop/acre comes Rs. 33,133. The major expenses come on threshing, weeding and harvesting. The cost of production /kg seed is Rs. 1,004. The seed yield of 33 kg / acre generates an income of Rs. 49,500/acre considering the seed price of Rs. 1,500. The cost of production can be reduced by introducing mechanization of threshing and winnowing.

SUGGESTIONS

Ramphal (1993) said that keeping in view highly perishable nature of flowers infrastructural facilities for post harvest handling and storage should be developed, policies of government should be made to eliminate dichotomy between production and marketing and incentive to the growers should be given to encourage them for export production. Appropriate steps are required to reduce airfreight and to make available adequate air cargo space to promote exports of floricultural products. Cheap green house technology suitable for Indian conditions may be developed. Regular interaction between researchers and floriculturists engaged in export will be beneficial in the development of export trade. High tech. flower growing facilities may be developed/established in and around cities with international airports so that flowers can be transported to important international markets.

Das and Mitra (1994) suggested that about forming of marketing co-operatives by the actual growers at village level, supply of qualitative seed materials, rural banks and other financial institutions should be liberal to provide credit to flower growers in time of need.

Singh (1994) suggested following strategies : identification of intensive floriculture zone, creation of appropriate infrastructure and suitable technology and equipment, making available on a large scale planting material and production inputs, adopting export specific market production, strengthening the market intelligence network, establishing service centers cum auction houses in potential zones, giving importance to product promotion activities and advertising creation and formation of cooperative florist organizations to safe guard the producers/ growers and enable them to control the marketing of their products and the government should support the industry as a whole and export oriented floriculture in particular.

Sindhu (1995) pointed out some suggestions to the interested farmers, investors, policy makers and research organizations especially those who are already engaged in the floricultural research projects, should come forward to take up the export oriented project on floriculture to meet the challenges before us.

Srivastava (1995) recommended that plant quarantine procedure should be simplified, reduce the tariff from 55 to 110 per cent on import without even import permit, reduce the import duties up to 25 per cent, subsidies on air-freight charges to the extent of 25 per cent, assistance from APEDA to the extent of 50 per cent of the cost of development of post harvest facilities, assistance from APEDA to the extent of 25 per cent of the cost of refrigerated transport unit, assistance on packaging, for using the material developed by APEDA to the extent of 30 per cent and 60 per cent and for market development and export promotion by APEDA. APEDA also assists in preparation of product promotion brochures and audio visual aids to the extent of 40 per cent.

Acharyya and Panda (1996) proposed glass house technology for production of export quality cut flowers, research on flower crops are to be intensified for establishing and promoting export trade in cut flowers, a unit with coolers and facilities for grading and packing near the cut flower growing areas is essential. An export promotion council should be set up.

Balasudhahari (1997) suggested that flowers should be harvested either in the early morning or in the late afternoon, as soon as the flowers are cut, the stems are placed in clean plastic buckets containing a clean solution of 500 ppm citric acid, time from grower to consumer should be shortest as possible. Sugar treatment improves flower opening and vase-life. It is particularly useful as a pre-treatment before export and is mainly for bud cut flowers. Grading should be done and then in packing extreme care should be taken. As soon as flowers are packed, they should be cooled down to optimum storage temperature. Refrigerated vehicle should be used to transport the cut flowers from farm to the airport.

Kundu *et al.* (1997) suggested that India should well develop glass house technology for production of export quality cut flower by growing selected exotic varieties which are already dominant in international market. Improvement in infrastructure facilities like cold storage at airport, refrigerated vans for transportation and units with cooling, grading and packaging facilities near the cut flower growing area is essential. Flowers exchange centers, an export promotion council should be set up for promoting floriculture exports. Well-developed marketing system should be set up. Airfreight duty charges should be abolished and there must be direct flights to importing countries keeping in view their perishable nature.

Maity (1997) emphasized that on creating better planting stock, better green house management and better cultural technology. The product left out below the export standard will find domestic market. In the state level a technical advisory board should be formed. Formation of a corporation is also necessary to develop floriculture. A change in the attitude of the policy makers is necessary to bring the floriculture to the forefront of agricultural crops.

Maity (1997) stressed on training part of flower cultivation. He said if a training programme in floriculture is at all hold, the time devoted is so brief that the subject can not be taken up in as much detail as would be helpful to the growers. The practical side of which should have the most important aspect of the training is mostly ignored.

In order to improve this situation the organizers themselves should first be convinced about the importance of floriculture. The training when held should give emphasis on the practical aspect. Demonstration fields have to be established for this purpose. Besides, only one important flower crop should be dealt at a time in the training, going in detail into various facts including production, post-harvest handling, storage, packing and marketing.

Sindhu and Misra (1997) concluded that the production technology must reach at the grass root level through effective extension network. The stock of well accepted varieties must be propagated sufficiently and distribution system should be strengthened. Efficient and viable production technology should be developed. The provision of bank loan on lower rate of interest may assist many floriculturists to take up production of flowers for export.

Marketing procedure of flowers should be channelized under the control of Government of India /State Government. Only elite planting material should be made available to the grower. The flowers should be grown according to their climate requirement. The government should decide support price for floricultural crops. At least two full-fledged institutes on floriculture should be established to strengthen the research back up. Some incentive in basic facilities, marketing, cargo space and cool chain must be given to the growers.

Apte and Bhargava (1998) proposed about building up an infrastructure development of climate-controlled stores and distribution centres, discuss the possibilities of bringing the export floriculture sector to the traditional horticulturist-farmer, support efforts of the APEDA to wholesale and auction markets in major cities, support the project like FMO-IPC-MSAMB project, to establish the all-India training institutes for the personnel and farmers in the floriculture sector.

Dahiya *et al.*(1999) concluded that until a dependable, quick and efficient marketing system i.e. export promotion policies, suitable price policies, processing production policies are framed the high profitability flowers may not be taken.

Ghosh (1999) said that large scale demonstrational training of extension functionaries to upgrade the skills for effective transfer of technology, setting up of collection centers and packaging houses at production sites, market information system, linking procedures and retailers with networking centers must receive urgent attention.

Chattopadhyay (2000) said that need of the day is awareness development through extension workers, field demonstration of advanced technology, liberal credit facilities, development of auction centers near the airports, cold storage for perishable flowers near the airports, extension of airfreight subsidy for floricultural items on international flights.

Dhawan (2002) reported that there is a need to popularize our own varieties in international market and obtain license for production of planting material both by conventional techniques and tissue culture of varieties, which are traded in international market. This will reduce the cost of planting material, utilizing the excess capacity of existing micro propagation laboratories and generating much needed employment.

Arora and Singh (2002) reported that selection of suitable cultivars, optimum growing temperatures and management's of crops are main factors which determine the post harvest quality of flowers. Flowers must be cut at a right stage of maturity. Cool chain to keep water loss as well as respiration at low ebb should be made an integral component of post harvest operations. Use of cheaper biocides should be promoted to extend flower longevity. The flowers of rose, gladiolus, tuberose should be harvested at bud stage since their buds continue to open in water, long vase-life, less sensitive to ethylene, easy to handle during storage, transport and are less prone to disease and pests.

Aforesaid literature indicate that studies have been conducted on importance of floriculture, its economics and constraints related to its adoption and one or other aspects of acceptability of flower cultivation technology in a fragmented manner. Whereas acceptability of any technology comprised of various stages like exposure, knowledge gain, attitude change, decision making for adoption, implementation on small scale and confirmation.

No study measure the potentiality of floriculture in terms of physical compatibility, cultural compatibility, profitability, trialability as an agribusiness, so this study is step forward in this direction.

A perusal of literature unfolds the fact that none of the study has given any attention to the acceptability of flower cultivation technology as a whole. The present study had made an attempt to incorporate all these parameters combined in the broader framework of acceptability along with constraints and factors affecting adoption and non-adoption by farm women. Therefore, in the present study all these components have been kept at appropriate place for exploration.

3

RESEARCH METHODOLOGY

Research methodology is study, descriptions explain and justification of methods, which aim at helping in understanding in the broadest possible terms not only the procedures of scientific enquiry but the process itself. It precisely describes the methodological steps, tools and instruments adopted in conducting the present investigation which have been presented under the following sections:

Exploring the Existing Pattern of Flower Cultivation Technology

For exploring the existing pattern of flower cultivation technology, the research procedure has been described under following heads:

1. *Locale of Study*

The study was carried out in Sonepat and Panipat districts of Haryana State because both the districts:

(i) are climatically best suited for flower cultivation;

(ii) have proximity to Delhi and well linked with train and road transportation where there is readily available national flower market.

2. *Exploration of Existing Flower Cultivation Pattern*

For exploration of existing pattern of flower cultivation technology in these districts, the researcher personally visited

District Horticulture office, DRDA office, Krishi Vigyan Kendra of Sonipat and Panipat districts, flower markets of both the districts and New Delhi and also explored relevant literature from Haryana Statistical Abstract (2001-2002) and collected following information:

— Area under flower cultivation in Haryana in the selected districts and villages separately.

— Sources of training/technical know how.

— Flowers/flower varieties grown.

— Source of finance

— Marketing of flowers

Imparting Technical Know How to Rural Women

For imparting technical know how/training in selected districts i.e. Sonepat and Panipat, research methodology procedure was adopted as:

HARYANCA STATE

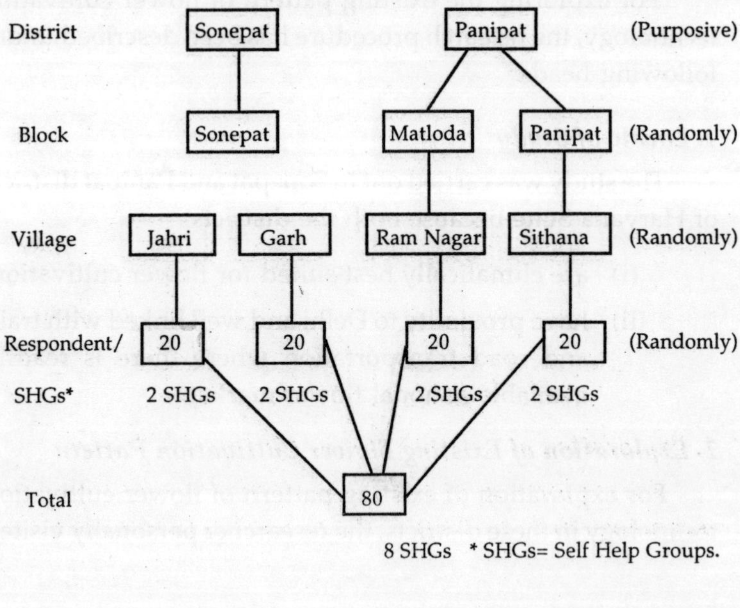

* SHGs= Self Help Groups.

1. *Sampling Procedure*

Multistage sampling procedure was adopted to select the respondents for the study.

(i) Selection of Blocks and Villages

From the selected districts, two blocks from Panipat comprising of one village from each block and from Sonepat district one block comprising of two villages were selected by random sampling procedure.

(ii) Selection of Respondents/ Self Help Groups

A list of total self help groups (SHGs) formed by Women Awareness and Management Agency (WAMA) in the selected villages was procured from the District project Manager, WAMA centre. Out of that list 2 SHGs/village (10 women in each group) were selected randomly, so as to have a sample of 80 rural farmwomen in 8 SHGs.

2. *Selection of Feasible Flowers/Flower Varieties*

To maintain continuity of the enterprise, a list of economically feasible flowers/flower varieties which could be grown round the year was prepared with the help of members of advisory committee, District Horticulture Officer, Govt. of Haryana at district level and out of this, chrysanthemum, marigold, gladiolus, rose and tuberose were selected.

3. *Development of Software*

A technical manual in Hindi on various messages related to flower cultivation technology was prepared in consultation with horticulture scientists and relevant literature, various massages included were:

— Concepts and importance

— Flowers/flower varieties

— Field preparation/sowing
— Transplantation
— Sowing/planting method & fertilizer application
— Plant protection
— Harvesting
— Packing and marketing
— Loaning facilities
— Precautions & limitations
— Overall knowledge

The language of the manual was purposively kept Hindi so as to suit the requirement of the rural women.

4. Organization of Training

Five days training on cultivation of selected economically feasible flowers was organized for a group of 20 women in 2 SHGs separately in each village in collaboration with experts of KVKs, department of District Horticulture Govt. of Haryana at district level with the help of lectures, demonstration and field visits. After training, prepared printed material was distributed to the respondents as a tool for future reference.

Analyzing the Acceptability Level of Flower Cultivation Enterprise

Acceptability of flower cultivation technology has been analysed under following sections:

1. Variables and Their Measurements

I. Independent Variables

A. Socio-Economic and Personal Variables

Variables	Instruments used
Age	Chronological age

Caste	Socio economic scaie (Rural) Kulshrestha (1980)
Education	Actual information
Family size	-do-
Land holding	-do-
Occupation	-do-
Income	-do-
Material possession	-do-

B. Communication Variables

Information source	**Inventory developed**
Mass media exposure	Kaur (1986)
Outside urban contact	Narwal (1981)

C. Economic Variables

Risk orientation	Supe (1969)
Economic motivation	Moulik (1965)
Innovation proneness	Moulik (1965)

D. Situational Variables

Cropping pattern	Kadian (1990)
Market access	Inventory developed

II. Dependent Variables

Acceptability of the technology	Rogers model of innovation decision process (1983)

I. Independent Variables

A. Socio-Economic and Personal Variables

Age

Age was operationalized as the chronological age of the

respondents and categorized as:

Categories	Score
19-29 years	1
30-40 years	2
41-51 years	3

Caste

Caste refers to for class or distinct hierarchy order of society. Respondents were classified into low, middle and high caste and score assigned to different caste groups were:

Caste		Score
Low:	Chamar, Bhangi, Dom,	1
	Jhimar,Khati, Dhobi, Badhi	2
Middle:	Lohar, Kumhar Tailor, Chippi,	3
	Baniya, Sonar, Ahir, Saini	4
High	Brahmin	5
	Jat, Rajput, Bishnoi	6

Education

It refers to years of formal education acquired by the respondents.

Family Type

It means whether it is a nuclear or a joint family. Nuclear family composed of members of only one person and includes minor and dependents, parents and children only. Joint family refers to one which is of two or more brother's family.

Family Size

It refers to total number of members in the family.

Land Holding

It refers to the land in acres possessed by the respondent's family. Following categories were made on the basis of the land holding.

Categories	**Score**
Upto 1 acre	1
2 to 5 acres	2
Above 5 acres	3

Occupation

It indicates the family's means of livelihood.

Income

Income was operationalized as the average monthly income earned by respondent's family. Categories formed and scores assigned were as follows:

Categories	**Scores**
Upto Rs.1000	1
Rs.1001-5000	2
Rs.5001 & above	3

Material Possession

It was operationalized in terms of household and improved agricultural implements goods and facilities possessed by the family of the respondents.

Socio-Economic Status

It is defined as position of the respondent in the society which is ascertained by various personal, social and economic variables. The score received by each respondent for each of the variable were added to estimate socio-economic status. The socio economic status scores were categorized into three categories as given follow:

Categorized	Score
Low (10-16)	1
Medium (17-23)	2
High (24-30)	3

B. Communication Variables

Information Source

This refers to the information sources used by respondents for obtaining required knowledge and information.

Mass Media Exposure

It refers to the degree to which a rural women has contact with mass media for obtaining the information on the required subject.

Outside Urban Contact

It has been operationalized as the contacts of an individual with the persons of urban areas/the visits performed by respondents outside the village for social and personal reason.

Extension Contact

It is degree of contact of the respondents with extension functionaries.

C. Economic Variables

Risk Orientation

It is degree to which a farmwomen is oriented towards risk and uncertainty and has the courage to face the problems.

Economic Motivation

It refers to the occupational success in terms of profit maximization and relative value placed by women on economic ends.

Innovation Proneness

It refers to the substitution of something new for another for growth of the society for a better living.

D. Situational/Variables

Cropping pattern

Market access

II. Dependent Variable

Acceptability of flower cultivation technology by farm women constituted the dependent variable. For the present study the acceptability was measured by taking into account the various parameters viz., knowledge, persuation, decision, implementation and confirmation as conceptualized by Rogers (1983) as shown in Fig.1.

Measurements of Parameters

Parameter	Measurement
Knowledge	Inventory developed
Persuation	Dogra (1988)
Decision	Inventory developed
Implementation	Inventory developed
Confirmation	Inventory developed

A. Knowledge

Knowledge has been operationalized as the amount of correct information possessed by the respondent regarding various messages of flower cultivation technology.

Aggregate scores were computed message-wise as well as overall knowledge score. Rural women's response on knowledge test obtained before and after training. On the basis of obtained scores knowledge level, knowledge gain, knowledge gap and knowledge index were computed.

Difference of post and pre exposure knowledge scores is knowledge gain. Difference of pre exposure to the maximum obtainable score and post exposure to the maximum obtainable score and then their individual difference drawn is knowledge gap.

Knowledge gain index (KGI) of each respondent was calculated by taking obtained knowledge gain (KGO) scores and maximum obtainable knowledge gain score (KGM).

$$KGI = \frac{KGO}{KGM} \times 100$$

The minimum score of knowledge gain index was 26.53 and the maximum was 40.82. Then respondents were categorized into three categories.

Categories	Range
Low	26.53 – 31.29
Medium	31.30 – 36.06
High	36.07 – 40.82

B. Persuation

It occurs when an individual forms a favourable or unfavourable attitude towards the innovation.

Thurstone (1946) defined attitude as the degree of positive or negative affect associated with some psychological object. By psychological object he meant any symbol, phrase, ideas, etc. towards which people can differ with respect to positive or negative affect. In this study, interpretation of attitude/ persuation was the same as suggested by Thusstone.

For measuring attitude of rural women towards flower cultivation technology, nineteen items were taken and each item in a scale was provided 3, 2, 1 score for positive statements and 1, 2, 3 for negative statements respectively. The total score of the respondents on the attitude scale was obtained by adding the scores, overall the individual items in the scale.

Responses of rural women's on attitude scale were obtained before and after training. On the basis of obtained scores attitude level, attitude change and attitude change index were calculated.

Attitude change index (ACI) for each respondent was calculated by using formula:

$$ACI = \frac{ACO}{ACM} \times 100$$

Where

ACO = Obtained attitude change score

ACM = Maximum obtainable attitude change score

The minimum score obtained of attitude change index was 3.92 and maximum was 52.96. The respondents were categorized in to three.

Categories	**Range**
Low	3.92 – 20.26
Medium	20.27 – 36.61
High	36.62 – 52.96

C. Decision

It refers to the stage when an individual engaged in activities that leads to a choice to adopt or reject the innovation. In the present study, decision-making has been operationalized as the extent to which recipients of technology, at first stage grasp and make mental decision to adopt or reject the adoption of flower cultivation technology.

Decision stage was analysed as:

(i) Statement-wise decision about implementation of the technology.

(ii) Attribute-wise decision about technology

(iii) Adoption feasibility index of the respondents.

(i) Statement-wise Decision

Decision-making was measured with the help of inventory developed. Rural women response on decision-making inventory was obtained only at one stage i.e. after the training. On the basis of obtained scores, decision about implementation of the technology was ascertained.

(ii) Attribute-wise Decision

It was assessed village-wise by taking into account the various attributes of innovation like:

(a) Relative advantage

(b) Cultural compatibility

(c) Situational compatibility

(d) Simplicity complexity

(e) Triability

(a) Relative Advantage

This was taken as degree to which the technology was perceived better and advantageous in terms of economic gains.

(b) Cultural Compatibility

This has been taken as degree to which an innovation was in agreement with belief and values of the respondents.

(c) Situational Compatibility

This has been taken as the degree to which technology was perceived as suitable to the agro-climatic conditions of the selected villages.

(d) Simplicity Complexity

This was operationalized as the degree to which technology is perceived as relatively easy/difficult to understand and use.

(c) Triability

This has been taken as the degree to which technology may be experimented on a small scale.

For all the above attributes the responses were obtained under five point rating scale and to assess attribute-wise decision of the respondents to implement the technology, mean scores were computed by adding the obtained scores for each of the attributes.

(iii) Adoption Feasibility Index (AFI)

Adoption feasibility index was computed by taking into account statement-wise as well as attribute-wise decision and formula used as:

$$AFI = \frac{AFO}{AFM} \times 100$$

Where,

AFO = Obtained score of adoption feasibility

AFM = Maximum obtainable score of adoption feasibility

The minimum score of adoption feasibility was 30.41 and the maximum was 100.00. Accordingly categories were formed:

Categories	Range
Low	30.41 – 53.61
Medium	53.62 – 76.80
High	76.81 – 100.00

D. Implementation

Implementation occurs when an individual puts an innovation into use on trial basis. It was analysed under following sub heads:

(i) Trial of technology

(ii) Implementation index

(i) Trial of Technology

To implement the technology three categories were formed on the basis of extent of adoption and scores assigned were:

Categories	Score
1. Adopter	
(a) Implemented immediately after training	3
(b) Adopted after 2-3 visits	2
2. Interested adopters	
(a) Interested but could not get required input	1
3. Non adopters	0

(ii) Implementation Index (II)

It was calculated by using the formula:

$$II = \frac{IO}{IM} \times 100$$

IO = Obtained score at implementation level

IM = Maximum obtainable score at implementation level and accordingly classes were formed.

Classes	Range
Low	2-34
Medium	35-67
High	68-100

Economical Feasibility (Potentiality)

Economic feasibility refers to the financial desirability of the project/technology for the smooth flow of the project/ technology/unit. To analyse the economic feasibility of the technology, it is essential to study cost of production i.e. operational cost, working cost, fixed cost and then cost and return analysis (cost benefit analysis).

Cost Benefit Analysis (Cost & Returns Analysis)

It was worked out after the implementation stage to find the economic feasibility of the technology as an incentive to rural women for actual adoption of the technology. It was measured on the basis of three costs i.e.

(i) Operational cost: it refers to cost incurred due to operational taking place in a crop cultivation.
(ii) Material cost: it is the cost of seed, fertilizer, manure, irrigation plant protection measure, interest on working cost and
(iii) Fixed cost: there are certain expenditure, which remain constant. They may represent cost of land rental value of land, transport, risk factor and management charges etc. required for the implementing technology.

Difference of gross return from total cost was the net income then per person income was calculated.

Income without taking into consideration rental value of land came out to be 'return over variable cost'. It was calculated for five crops individually.

E. Confirmation

It refers to the stage when an individual seeks reinforcement of the innovation decision already made.

Confirmation was analysed as:

(i) Adoption of technology

(ii) Adoption index.

(i) Adoption of Technology

On the basis of extent of actual adoption, respondents were categorized into three categories as:

	Categories	Score
1.	Adopted immediately after completion of 1st crop	3
2.	Adopter after seeing the profit of 1st group	2
3.	Adopted after seeing profit and further motivation	1
4.	Not at all adopted	0

(ii) Adoption Index (AI)

It was computed by formula:

$$AI = \frac{AO}{AM} \times 100$$

AO = Obtained score at adoption level

AM = Maximum obtainable score at adoption level

Accordingly categories formed:

Categories	**Range**
Low	2-34
Medium	35-67
High	68 – 100

2. *Overall Acceptability of the Technology*

For assessing the overall acceptability of the technology, acceptability index was calculated. Acceptability index has been operationalized as the sum total of obtained scores (AO_1) of knowledge gain, attitude change, decision, implementation and confirmation of the technology by the respondents divided by their maximum obtainable scores (AM_1) at each stage respectively and multiply by 100. The acceptability index (AI_1) was computed by the formula:

$$AI_1 = \frac{AO_1}{AM_1} \times 100$$

AO_1 = Obtained score at acceptability level

AI_1 = Acceptability index

AM_1 = Maximum obtainable scores

3. *Construction of Interview Schedule*

The structured interview schedule was prepared in accordance with the methodological procedure described. It was duly pretested on 30 non sampled respondents accordingly modification and corrections were incorporated to make the instrument functional.

4. *Collection of Data*

For the first two steps i.e. knowledge and persuation data were collected both at pre and post exposure stage where as data regarding decision, implementation, confirmation, constraints, factors affecting adoption and non-adoption of flower cultivation technology were collected only after training.

5. *Analysis and Interpretation of Data*

The qualitative data were quantified according to the

standards laid down and tabulated to draw inferences. Statistical tools applied were as follows:

Tests/measures used		Purpose
1. Percentage	—	Profile variables of respondents
	—	Pre and post knowledge, gain in knowledge, knowledge gap and attitude level.
	—	Decision about implementation, adoption feasibility, reasons for non-adoption
	—	Constraints in adoption
	—	Cost and return analysis
	—	Confirmation
2. Mean scores, Rank	—	Pre and post knowledge
	—	Knowledge gap
	—	Adoption feasibility
3. Index	—	Knowledge gain index
	—	Attitude change index
	—	Adoption feasibility index
	—	Implementation index
	—	Confirmation index
	—	Overall acceptability index
4. Correlation co-efficient	—	To assess the relationship among the variables
5. Multiple regre-ssion	—	To predict the value of dependent variables from 2 more independent variables combined.

On the basis of statistical test, interpretations of results was done, inferences and conclusions were drawn.

4

RESULT AND DISCUSSION

This chapter pertains to the results and discussion based on the findings of the study. The results and discussion in accordance with the objectives of the study are presented as under:

Existing Pattern of Flower Cultivation Technology

The information regaridng the existing pattern of flower cultivation technology was gathered through the secondary sources like District Horticulture Office (DHO), Krishi Vigyan Kendra (KVK), District Rural Development Agency (DRDA), flower market of Sonepat and Panipat districts, National Horticulture office, progressive farmers and from relevant literature.

A. Area (ha) Under Cultivation

The flower cultivation area was higher in Sonepat (670 ha) in comparison to Panipat (145 ha) district. The marigold cultivation area was higher covering 450 and 120 ha followed by 150 and 10 ha under rose in both Sonepat and Panipat districts respectively. The chrysanthemum, gladiolus and tuberose were found to be grown in 25, 20 and 10 ha respectively in Sonepat district. In Panipat district, the gladiolus cultivation was on five ha but have no area under chrysanthemum and tuberose. Regarding villages i.e. Jahri & Garh in Sonepat district, Rose was grown on 40 ha in Jahri & 42 ha in Garh village followed by marigold i.e. 7 & 15 ha respectively, whereas gladiolus was grown on 3 & 1 ha respectively. In Sithana and Ram Nagar village, there was no area under flower cultivation during 2001-02.

B. Commercial Varieties Grown

Main varieties of rose cultivation were found to be desi gulab, bulgarian roses, rakt gandha, yellamera and crimson. Gladiolus was grown mainly in three colours i.e. white, red and blue.

(i) The white coloured gladiolus varieties were 'white prosperity', 'friendship', 'American beauty', 'vincus glory' and a local variety called 'appolo'.

(ii) The red coloured varieties were 'red magisty' and 'oscar'.

(iii) The blue coloured gladiolus varieties were 'her majesty'and 'mayure'.

The chrysanthemum varieties grown were 'single' (white) and 'market' (local variety). Similarly the tuberose varieties grown were single and double (white). The African marigold varieties were 'African giant' (both in red and yellow colour) and French marigold varieties were 'rusty red' and local.

The DHO and KVK provided technical guidance from time to time. In the villages where already flower cultivation was there, these farm women got knowledge from progressive farmers. Easy availability of loan was availed through credit cards, banks and DRDA but private financing was main source of loan. Local market of Sonepat and Panipat districts in Haryana and Connaught Place and Khari Bawli in New Delhi were used for marketing purpose.

Imparting Technical Know How and Analyzing the Acceptability Level of Flower Cultivation Enterprise

Training's on flower cultivation technology were

organized for rural women in all the selected villages under study and the acceptability of technology was assessed in terms of knowledge gain, knowledge gap, attitude change, decision making, implementation and confirmation about adoption. Accordingly analysis was done under the following sub-sections:

1. *Profile Variables of the Respondents*

Profile of the respondents was prepared and presented in Table2 based on personal, socio-economic, communication and situational variables.

TABLE 1

The Existing Pattern of Flower Cultivation in Selected Districts and Villages (2001-2002)

	India - Land Under Flower cultivation.		*88607 ha*			
	Districts		*Villages*			
	Sonepat	*Panipat*	*Jahri*	*Garh*	*Sithana*	*Ram Nagar*
A. Area (ha)						
Area under floriculture	670	145	51	63	Nil	Nil
Rose	150	15	40	42	Nil	Nil
Gladiolus	20	4	3	1	Nil	Nil
Chrysanthemum	25	Nil	Nil	Nil	Nil	Nil
Tuberose	10	Nil	Nil	Nil	Nil	Nil
Marigold	450	120	7	15	Nil	Nil
Others like chameli, kaner, mogra	15	6	1	5	Nil	Nil

B. Crop	**Commercial varieties grown**
Rose (*Rosa indica*)	Desi Gulab Bulgarian roses Rakt Gandha

	Yellamera
	Crimson
Gladiolus (*Gladiolus* grandiflours L.)	**White**
	White Prosperity
	Friendship
	American Beauty
	Vincus Glory
	Appolo (Local variety)
	Red
	Red Magisty
	Oscar
	Blue
	Her majesty
	Mayure
Chrysanthemum (*Chrysanthemum morifolium* Ramat.)	Single (white)
	Market (Local variety)
Tuberose (*Polianthes tuberosa* L.)	Single & double (White)
Marigold (*Tagetes erecta* L.)	**African**
	African Giant (Red & Yellow)
	French
	Rusty Red
	Local
C. Technical guidance/Knowledge	District Horticulture Office (DHO)
	Krshi Vigyan Kendra (KVK)
	Progressive Farmers
D. Sources of finance (loan/ subsidy)	Credit card
	District Rural Development Agency
	Banks
	Private financing agencies
E. Marketing of flowers	Sonepat & Panipat local market, Connaught Palace & Khari Bawli (Delhi)

Sources District Horticulture Office (DHO)
Krishi Vigyan Kendra of Sonepat & Panipat districts
Haryana Statistical Abstract (2001-2002)
Flower markets of Sonepat, Panipat and also Delhi
Progressive farmers

TABLE 2

Profile of the Respondents

Sr. No.	Variables	*Districts*				Total N = 80
		Sonipat		*Panipat*		
		Jahri n=20	*Garh n=20*	*Sithana n=20*	*Ram Nagar n=20*	
1	**Age**					
	(a) 19-29 years	6(30)	7(35)	10(50)	6(30)	29(36.25)
	(b) 30-40 years	10(50)	9(45)	8(40)	12(60)	39(48.75)
	(c) 41-51 years	4(20)	4(20)	2(10)	2(10)	12(15.00)
2.	**Caste**					
	(a) Low	0(0)	3(15)	20(100)	20(100)	43(53.75)
	(b) Middle	2(10)	11(55)	0(0)	0(0)	13(16.25)
	(c) High	18(90)	6(30)	0(0)	0(0)	24(30.00)
3.	**Family type**					
	(a) Nuclear	14(70)	11(55)	18(90)	15(75)	58(72.50)
	(b) Joint	6(30)	9(45)	2(10)	5(25)	22(27.50)
4.	**Family size**					
	(a) Small (upto 4)	4(20)	4(20)	7(35)	3(15)	18(22.50)
	(b) Medium (5-8)	11(55)	9(45)	11(55)	17(85)	48(60.00)
	(c) Large (above 8)	5(25)	7(35)	2(10)	0(0)	14(17.50)
5.	**Land holding**					
	(a) Upto 1 acre	8(40)	14(70)	9(45)	12(60)	43(53.75)
	(b) 2-5 acre	8(40)	6(30)	2(10)	5(25)	21(26.25)
	(c) Above 5 acre	4(20)	0(0)	9(45)	3(15)	16(20.00)
6.	**Occupation**					
	(a) Farming	2(10)	11(55)	4(20)	9(45)	26(32.50)
	(b) Business/service	0(0)	0(0)	0(0)	0(0)	0(0)
	(c) Labour	0(0)	0(0)	0(0)	0(0)	0(0)
	(d) Farming and Business/service	18(90)	8(40)	1(5)	2(10)	29(36.25)
	(e) Farming & Labour	0(0)	1(5)	15(75)	9(45)	25(31.25)

7. Education					
(a) Illiterate	6(30)	5(25)	13(65)	7(35)	31(38.75)
(b) Primary	4(20)	3(15)	5(25)	6(30)	18(22.50)
(c) Middle	1(5)	7(35)	0(0)	0(0)	8(10.00)
(d) High School	8(40)	5(25)	1(5)	7(35)	21(26.25)
(e) Graduate and above	1(5)	0(0)	1(5)	0(0)	2(2.50)
8. Income					
(a) Low (upto 1000)	1(5)	8(40)	10(50)	10(50)	29(36.25)
(b) Middle (1001-5000)	12(60)	7(35)	7(35)	6(30)	32(40.00)
(c) High (above 5001)	7(35)	5(25)	3(15)	4(20)	9(11.25)
9. Material possession					
(a) Low (2-21)	11(55)	15(75)	14(70)	6(30)	46(57.50)
(b) Medium (22-41)	6(30)	5(25)	2(10)	11(55)	24(30.00)
(c) High (42-61)	3(15)	0(0)	4(20)	3(15)	10(12.50)
10. Socio-economic status					
(a) Low (10-16)	0(0)	5(25)	11(55)	11(55)	27(33.75)
(b) Medium (17-23)	14(70)	13(65)	8(40)	9(45)	44(55.00)
(c) High (24-30)	6(30)	2(10)	1(5)	0(0)	9(11.25)
11. Communication variables					
(a) Low (1-9)	14(70)	15(75)	13(65)	1(5)	43(53.75)
(b) Medium (10-18)	5(25)	5(25)	7(35)	15(75)	32(40.00)
(c) High (19-27)	1(5)	0(0)	0(0)	4(20)	5(6.25)
12 Economical variables					
(i) Innovation proneness					
(a) Low (9-12)	0(0)	0(0)	0(0)	20(100)	20(25.00)
(b) Medium (13-16)	5(25)	6(30)	18(90)	0(0)	29(36.25)
(c) High (17-20)	15(75)	14(70)	2(10)	0(0)	31(38.75)
(ii) Risk orientation					
(a) Low (10-13)	0(0)	0(0)	0(0)	20(100)	20(25.00)
(b) Medium (14-17)	0(0)	5(25)	14(70)	0(0)	19(23.75)
(c) High (18-21)	20(100)	15(75)	6(30)	0(0)	41(51.25)
(iii) Economic motivation					
(a) Low (11-13)	0(0)	0(0)	0(0)	10(50)	10(12.50)
(b) Medium (14-16)	11(55)	9(45)	18(90)	10(50)	48(60.00)
(c) High (17-19)	9(45)	11(55)	2(10)	0(0)	22(27.50)

(iv)	**Consideration of situational variables**					
(a)	Never	3(15)	10(50)	0(0)	4(20)	17(21.25)
(b)	Some times	10(50)	10(50)	18(90)	4(20)	42(52.50)
(c)	Always	7(35)	0(0)	2(10)	12(60)	21(26.25)

Figures in parentheses indicate percentages.

Age

The table depicted that majority (48.75%) of the rural women were in middle age group i.e. 30-40 years, followed by young, i.e. 19-29 years (36.25%) and remaining (15.00%) were in above 41 years age.

Caste

Caste wise distribution of the respondents shows that 53.75 per cent women belonged to low caste followed by high (30.00%) and middle (16.25%).

Family Type

It was found that 72.50 per cent respondents belonged to nuclear type family system followed by joint type (27.50%).

Family Size

The data presented in table 2 shows that majority (60.00%) of the women had medium family size followed by small (22.50%) and large (17.50%).

Land Holding

The result concerned with land holding depicted that little more than half of the respondents (53.75%) had land upto 1 acre, followed by 2-5 acre (26.25%) and above 5 acre (20.00%).

Occupation

The farming was the main occupation of all the respondents (100.00%) followed by business/service and labour.

Education

The majority (61.25%) of respondents had education upto primary level followed by high school (26.25%), middle (10.00%) and graduate (2.50%) level.

Income

It is well exhibited in table2 that 40 per cent respondents belonged to middle income group followed by low (36.25%) and high (11.25%).

Material Possession

It is evident from the data that more than half (57.50 %) of the respondents had low material possession followed by middle (30.00%) and high (12.50%).

Socio-economic Status

The data pertaining to socio-economic status revealed that in general 55.00 per cent respondents had medium socio-economic status. It was followed by low (33.75%) and high (11.25%).

Communication Variables

It is apparent from the data that exposure of rural farm women to communication sources was found to be low in more than half of the respondents (53.75%) followed by medium (44.00%) and high (6.25%).

Economic Variables

(i) Innovation Proneness

The data pertaining to table2 shows that majority of the respondent's fall from high (38.75%) to medium (36.25%) level of innovation proneness. It was followed by low (25.00%) level.

(ii) Risk Orientation

Little more than half (51.25%) of the respondents had higher risk taking capacity followed by low (25.00%) and high (23.75%).

(iii) Economic Motivation

It is observed that 60.00 per cent respondents were economically motivated towards technology followed by high (27.50%) and low (12.50%).

Situational Variables

For choosing any type of cropping pattern or farming system more than half (52.50%) of the respondents took situational variables into consideration followed by high (26.25 %) and low (21.25%).

Thus, it can be inferred from the results of the study that 48.75 per cent respondents belonged to middle age group, low caste (53.75%) having nuclear type of family system (72.50%) and medium family size (60.00%). Regarding economic variables 53.75 per cent had upto 1 acre land. Farming (100.00%) as main occupation, illiterate (38.75%) belonged to medium income group (40.00%) and having low (57.50%) material possession. More than half of the rural farm women had medium socio-economic status, low (53.75%) communication exposure, high innovation proneness (38.75%), high risk orientation (51.25%) and medium economic motivation (60.00). More than half (52.50%) of the respondents taken care of medium level of situational variables.

2. *Knowledge Level of the Respondents about Flower Cultivation Technology*

Knowledge level about flower cultivation technology was analysed under following sub-sections:

1. Pre and Post Exposure Knowledge Level

The knowledge of the respondents regarding flower cultivation technology at pre and post-exposure level was ascertained message wise as well as technology as a whole. For message-wise analysis, 10 items were selected viz. concepts and importance, flowers/flower varieties, field preparation/

TABLE 3

Pre and Post Knowledge in Flower Cultivation Technology

Sr. No.	Message Categories	Pre-exposure					Post-exposure				
		Districts				Total N=80	Districts				Total N=80
		Sonipat		Panipat			Sonipat		Panipat		
		Jahri n=20	Garh n=20	Sithana n=20	Ram Nagar n=20		Jahri n=20	Garh n=20	Sithana n=20	Ram Nagar n=20	
1.	**Concepts and importance**										
	Low (5-9)	16(80)	5(25)	12(60)	14(70)	47(58.75)	0(0)	0(0)	0(0)	0(0)	0(0.00)
	Medium (10-14)	4(20)	7(35)	8(40)	6(30)	25(31.25)	3(15)	2(10)	7(35)	5(25)	17(21.25)
	High (15-19)	0(0)	8(40)	0(0)	0(0)	8(10.00)	18(90)	13(65)	13(65)	15(75)	63(78.75)
2	**Flowers/flower varieties**										
	Low (1-5)	20(100)	20(100)	20(100)	20(100)	80(100.00)	0(0)	0(0)	0(0)	0(0)	0(0.00)
	Medium (6-10)	0(0)	0(0)	0(0)	0(0)	0(0.00)	20(100)	20(100)	20(100)	20(100)	80(100.00)
	High (11-15)	0(0)	0(0)	0(0)	0(0)	0(0.00)	0(0)	0(0)	0(0)	0(0)	0(0.00)
3.	**Field preparation/ sowing**										
	Low (0-2)	18(90)	8(40)	20(100)	16(80)	62(77.50)	3(15)	13(65)	3(15)	6(30)	25(31.25)

Medium (3-5)	2(10)	12(60)	0(0)	4(20)	18(22.50)	15(75)	7(35)	17(65)	14(70)	53(66.25)
High (6-8)	0(0)	0(0)	0(0)	0(0)	0(0.00)	2(10)	0(0)	0(0)	0(0)	2(2.50)
4. Transplantation										
Low (0-2)	20(100)	16(80)	20(100)	17(85)	73(91.25)	12(60)	17(85)	13(65)	14(70)	56(70.00)
Medium (3-5)	0(0)	4(20)	0(0)	3(15)	7(8.75)	8(40)	3(15)	7(35)	6(30)	24(30.00)
High (6-8)	0(0)	0(0)	0(0)	0(0)	0(0.00)	0(0)	0(0)	0(0)	0(0)	0(0.00)
5 Sowing/planting method & fertilizer application										
Low (0-2)	20(100)	20(100)	20(100)	20(100)	80(100.00)	20(100)	20(100)	20(100)	20(100)	80(100.00)
Medium (3-5)	0(0)	0(0)	0(0)	0(0)	0(0.00)	0(0)	0(0)	0(0)	0(0)	0(0.00)
High (6-8)	0(0)	0(0)	0(0)	0(0)	0(0.00)	0(0)	0(0)	0(0)	0(0)	0(0.00)
6. Plant protection										
Low (0-1)	20(100)	20(100)	20(100)	20(100)	80(100.00)	14(70)	6(30)	9(45)	12(60)	41(51.25)
Medium (2-3)	0(0)	0(0)	0(0)	0(0)	0(0.00)	6(30)	14(70)	11(55)	8(40)	39(48.75)
High (4-5)	0(0)	0(0)	0(0)	0(0)	0(0.00)	0(0)	0(0)	0(0)	0(0)	0(0.00)
7. Harvesting										
Low (0-2)	20(100)	20(100)	20(100)	20(100)	80(100.00)	20(100)	7(35)	13(65)	19(95)	59(73.75)
High (2-4)	0(0)	0(0)	0(0)	0(0)	0(0.00)	0(0)	13(65)	7(35)	1(5)	21(26.25)
8. Packing and marketing										
Low (0-4)	20(100)	20(100)	20(100)	20(100)	80(100.00)	0(0)	0(0)	0(0)	0(0)	0(0.00)
Medium (5-9)	0(0)	0(0)	0(0)	0(0)	0(0.00)	20(100)	20(100)	20(100)	20(100)	80(100.00)

High (10-15)	0(0)	0(0)	0(0)	0(0)	0(0.00)	0(0)	0(0)	0(0)	0(0)	0(0.00)
9 **Loaning facilities**										
Low (0-2)	20(100)	20(100)	20(100)	20(100)	80(100.00)	10(50)	2(10)	5(25)	10(50)	27(33.75)
Medium (3-4)	0(0)	0(0)	0(0)	0(0)	0(0.00)	10(50)	18(90)	15(75)	10(50)	53(66.25)
High (5-6)	0(0)	0(0)	0(0)	0(0)	0(0.00)	0(0)	0(0)	0(0)	0(0)	0(0.00)
10. **Precautions & limitations**										
Low (1-3)	19(75)	20(100)	14(70)	12(60)	65(81.25)	0(0)	0(0)	0(0)	0(0)	0(0.00)
Medium (4-6)	1(5)	0(0)	6(30)	8(40)	15(18.75)	20(100)	20(100)	20(100)	20(100)	80(100.00)
High (7-9)	0(0)	0(0)	0(0)	0(0)	0(0.00)	0(0)	0(0)	0(0)	0(0)	0(0.00)
11. **Overall knowledge**										
Low (9-26)	20(100)	9(45)	20(100)	17(85)	66(82.50)	0(0)	0(0)	0(0)	0(0)	0(0.00)
Medium (26-43)	0(0)	11(55)	0(0)	3(15)	14(17.50)	3(15)	2(10)	1(5)	3(15)	9(11.25)
High (43-60)	0(0)	0(0)	0(0)	0(0)	0(0.00)	17(85)	18(90)	19(95)	17(85)	71(88.75)

Figures in parantheses indicate percentages.

sowing, transplantation, sowing/planting method & fertilizer application, plant protection, harvesting, packing and marketing, loaning facilities and precautions & limitations. The respondents were categorized into three groups i.e. low, medium and high on the knowledge scores they obtained on most of the messages of flower cultivation technology except harvesting where only two categories i.e. high and low were formed. Data from table2 shows that majority (82.50%) of the respondents were found to have overall as well as message-wise low knowledge level about flower cultivation technology followed by medium level (17.50%) of knowledge at pre-exposure level. Regarding flower/flower varieties, sowing/planting method & fertilizer application, plant protection, harvesting, packing & marketing, loaning facilities messages, cent per cent respondents had no knowledge followed by low level of knowledge on field preparation/sowing (77.50%), transplantation (91.25%) and precaution& limitations (81.25%) at pre-exposure level. But after training, the respondents had high knowledge in concepts & importance (78.75%) followed by medium knowledge level in respect to flower/ flower varieties (100.00%), field preparation/sowing (66.25%), packaging and marketing (100.00%), loaning facilities (66.25%), precautions and limitations (100.00%). Respondents (70.00%) had low knowledge level in transportation, sowing/planting method and fertilizer application (100.00%), plant protection (51.25%), harvesting (73.75%), on flower cultivation technology. It may be due to illiteracy of the majority of women and also because, these messages include highly technical knowledge. Overall knowledge level of the respondents was high (88.75%) followed by medium (11.25%) at post-exposure stage.

TABLE 4

Knowledge Gain in Flower Cultivation Technology

S. No.	*Massage/Categories*	*Villagewise respondents*				*Total (n = 80)*
		Jahri (n=20)	*Garh (n=20)*	*Sithana (n=20)*	*Ram Nagar (n=20)*	
1.	**Concept and important**					
	Low (1-4)	0(0)	8(40)	0(0)	0(0)	8(10.00)
	Medium (5-8)	10(50)	11(55)	17(85)	12(60)	50(62.50)
	High (9-12)	10(50)	1(5)	3(15)	8(40)	22(27.50)
2.	**Flowers/flower varieties**					
	Low (4-5)	3(15)	0(0)	0(0)	5(25)	8(10.00)
	Medium (6-7)	8(40)	12(60)	9(45)	8(40)	37(46.25)
	High (8-9)	9(45)	8(40)	11(55)	7(35)	35(43.75)
3.	**Field preparation and sowing/planting time**					
	Low (1-2)	3(15)	13(65)	3(15)	6(30)	25(31.25)
	Medium (3-4)	8(40)	5(25)	16(80)	13(65)	42(52.50)
	High (5-6)	9(45)	2(10)	1(5)	1(5)	13(16.25)
5.	**Transplantation**					
	Low (0-2)	12(60)	16(80)	13(65)	14(70)	55(68.75)
	High (3-4)	8(40)	4(20)	7(35)	6(30)	25(31.25)
6.	**Sowing/planting method and fertilizer application**					
	Low (0-1)	10(50)	18(90)	12(60)	15(75)	55(68.75)
	High (1-2)	10(50)	2(10)	8(40)	5(25)	25(31.25)
7.	**Plant protection**					
	Low (0-1)	14(70)	8(40)	9(45)	12(60)	43(53.75)
	High (1-2)	6(30)	12(60)	11(55)	8(40)	37(46.25)
8.	**Harvesting**					
	Low (0-1)	9(45)	6(30)	5(25)	11(55)	31(38.75)
	High (1-2)	11(55)	14(70)	15(75)	9(45)	49(61.25)
9.	**Packing & marketing**					
	Low (3-4)	3(15)	13(65)	7(35)	5(25)	28(35.00)

Medium (4-5)	10(50)	4(20)	9(45)	7(35)	30(37.50)
High (5-6)	7(35)	3(15)	4(20)	8(40)	22(27.50)
10. Loaning facilities					
Low (1-2)	10(50)	2(10)	4(20)	7(35)	23(28.75)
Medium (2-3)	10(50)	11(55)	9(45)	13(65)	43(53.75)
High (3-4)	0(0)	7(35)	7(35)	0(0)	14(17.50)
11. Precautions & limitations					
Low (0-1)	4(20)	3(15)	6(30)	6(30)	19(23.75)
High (2-3)	16(80)	17(85)	14(70)	14(70)	61(76.25)

Figures in parentheses indicate percentages.

Thus, results lead to conclusion that at post-exposure stage, majority of the respondents had sufficient knowledge about flower cultivation technology. It may be due to the fact that respondents were convinced about the profitability, social & cultural compatibility and triability of the project technology i.e. flower cultivation technology.

Knowledge Gain

In order of statistical test, the significance of gain in knowledge, the mean score of respondents were compared before and after exposure of training by the use of paired 't' test. For each of the respondent, training score for each message as well as aggregate scores of the whole training were compared for pre-exposure and post-exposure knowledge. The comparative mean scores of the respondents and value of 't' test as applied is shown in Table 6.

It is evident from the table that 't' values were found to be significant at five per cent level of significance for all messages except fertilizer application due to highly technical nature of this message, which revealed that there was significant difference in knowledge of rural women at pre & post-exposure stage. It means all the respondents gained statistically significant knowledge after exposure except in fertilizer application message.

Change in Knowledge Gap in Flower Cultivation Messages

Knowledge gap refers to the difference in amount of information rural women possessed about different messages of flower cultivation and the amount of information which was given through training, knowledge gap in the present study was assessed before and after the rural women were exposed to training in order to determine the reduction in knowledge gap. Analysis of the knowledge gap was done and message wise data are furnished in Table 5.

TABLE 5

Change in Knowledge Gap in Flower Cultivation Technology

Sr. No.	*Messages*	*Pre-exposrue Knoweldge gap score*	*Knowledge gap difference*	*Post-exposure knowledge gap score*	*Maximum attainable score*
1	Concept and importance	14.95 (62.29)	(32.08)	7.25 (30.21)	24
2.	Flowers/flower varieties	11.26 (86.64)	(48.76)	4.93 (37.88)	13
3.	Field preparation and sowing/ planting time	3.26 (72.09)	(37.40)	1.56 (34.59)	4
4.	Transplantation	6.74 (84.22)	(16.72)	5.40 (67.50)	8
5.	Sowing/planting method and fertilizer application	3.48 (99.36)	(10.32)	3.07 (89.04)	3.5
6.	Plant protection	5.00 (100.00)	(29.50)	3.53 (70.50)	5
7.	Harvesting	6.24 (89.11)	(7.50)	5.71 (81.61)	7

8.	Packing and marketing	10.93 (91.04)	(41.04)	6.00 (50.00)	12
9.	Loaning facilities	6.00 (100.00)	(38.13)	3.71 (61.88)	6
10.	Precautions and limitations	2.45 (61.25)	(25.00)	1.45 (36.25)	4
11.	Overall knowledge	7.03 (84.60)	(28.65)	4.26 (55.95)	86.5

Figures in parentheses indicate corresponding percentages.

Concept and Importance

At pre-exposure stage, the knowledge gap with respect to concept and importance of flower cultivation was found 69.29 per cent and at post-training stage gap was reduced to 30.21 per cent. The knowledge gap difference between pre and post-exposure was found 32.08 per cent.

Flower/Flower Varieties

For kinds of flowers/flower varieties message gap at pre-training stage was 86.64 per cent and at post-exposure stage, the knowledge gap was 37.88 per cent. The knowledge gap difference between pre and post exposure of training was found to be 48.76 per cent, which revealed maximum knowledge gap difference still, exist in flower/flower varieties.

Field Preparation and Sowing/Planting Time

The perusal of the table 5 brings forth the fact that existing knowledge gap of trainees with respect field preparation and sowing/planting time was 72.09 per cent. At post-exposure stage knowledge gap of rural women was 34.59 per cent. The gap difference was observed to be 37.40 per cent.

TABLE 6

Mean Score of Pre and Post-exposure Knowledge Gain of Respondents

S. No.	*Massages*	*Mean knowledge*		
		Pre-exposure	*Post-exposure*	*'t' values*
1.	Concept & importance	9.000	17.050	19.695*
2.	Flower/flower varieties	1.738	7.988	53.270*
3.	Field preparation	1.063	1.513	6.553*
4.	Sowing/planting time	0.538	3.413	27.565*
5.	Transplantation	1.213	2.588	10.031*
6.	Sowing/planting method	0.025	0.825	8.156*
7.	Fertilizer application	0.025	0.050	1.423
8.	Plant protection	0.000	1.488	25.219*
9.	Harvesting	0.763	2.388	18.502*
10.	Packing & marketing	1.075	5.963	51.024*
11.	Loaning facilities	0.000	2.838	35.278*
12.	Precautions & limitations	1.500	2.551	17.179*

* Significant at 5 per cent level of significance

Transplantation

The knowledge gap was 84 per cent among the respondents for transplantation message at pre-training stage, whereas, it was 67.50 per cent at post-exposure stage. The knowledge gap difference was revealed to be 16.72 per cent.

Sowing/Planting Method and Fertilizer Application

With regard to practices related to sowing/planting method and fertilizer application, knowledge gap difference was found to be 10.32 per cent between pre and post-exposure whereas, knowledge gap was 99.36 and 89.04 per cent at pre and post-exposure stages respectively.

Plant Protection

The data in the Table 5 highlighted that the initial knowledge of the respondents with respect to plant protection message was nil as indicated by the pre-exposure knowledge gap (100%). Post exposure level of knowledge gap (72.50%) indicated knowledge gap difference of 29.50 per cent.

Harvesting

Regarding harvesting massage, trainees knowledge gap at pre-exposure stage was 89.11 per cent. But at post exposure stage, it reduced to 81.61 per cent. A little difference of 7.50 per cent was observed at pre and post exposure training stage. The reason for this result was that half of the respondents did not see even field of flower crop.

Packing and Marketing

Fifty per cent knowledge gap was observed in post exposure stage whereas, it was 91.04 per cent in pre exposure stage. A significant knowledge gap difference (41.04%) was observed due to training.

Loaning Facilities

At pre-exposure stage, initial knowledge was nil, it means there was 100.00 per cent knowledge gap, however, in post exposure stage due to training, it was reduced to 61.88 per cent indicating thereby 38.13 per cent knowledge gap difference.

Precautions and Limitations

At pre-exposure stage with respect to precautions and limitation, knowledge gap was observed as 61.25 per cent. But at post-exposure, knowledge gap was reduced to 36.25 per cent. The knowledge gap difference between pre and post exposure was found to be 25.00 per cent.

The data in table5 clearly indicated that the knowledge gap was above 84 and 55.95 per cent on an average both at pre-exposure stage and at post exposure stage respectively. This indicates results of training except on harvesting and sowing/planting method and fertilizer application message, where no significant knowledge gap difference was observed. It may be due to illiteracy of women and highly technical and practical nature of both the messages.

4. Knowledge Gain

Knowledge gain with respect to difference between pre-exposure and post-exposure knowledge level of farm women about flower cultivation messages is presented in table 4. The data revealed the high knowledge gain in the messages: harvesting (61.25%) and precautions and limitations (76.25%). Medium knowledge gain in concept and importance (62.50%), flowers/flower varieties (46.25%), field preparation & sowing/planting time (52.75%), packing & marketing (37.50%) and loaning facilities (53.75%) followed this. In messages like transplantation (68.75%) sowing/planting time & fertilizer application (68.75%) and plant protection (53.75%), the low knowledge gain was due to technical nature of the messages and illiteracy of the majority of the respondents.

From the above findings, it can be inferred that the training on flower cultivation technology helped the respondents to gain knowledge. These results are in the line as were in the study of Anita (2000). These may be due to the reason that in both the cases respondents were interested due to profitability and suitability of the technology.

5. Knowledge Gain Index

Knowledge gain index calculated with the help of formula explained in the methodology and the results were indicated in table 7.

TABLE 7

Knowledge gain index

S. No.	Categories (n=20)	Jahri (n=20)	Garh (n=20)	Sithana (n=20)	Ram Nagar (n=20)	Total (n=80)
		Village-wise respondents				
1.	Low (26.53-31.29)	5(25)	13(65)	4(20)	7(35)	29(36.25)
2.	Medium (32.29-37.06)	9(45)	6(30)	13(65)	11(55)	39(48.75)
3.	High (38.06-41.82)	6(30)	1(5)	3(15)	2(10)	12(15.00)

Figures in parentheses indicate percentages

It is noted that maximum numbers of the respondents (48.75%) fall in the category of medium knowledge gain index. This was followed by low (36.25%) where as only 15.00 per cent respondent were having high knowledge gain index. This helped in indicating clearly knowledge gain due to exposure of rural women through training.

3. *Attitude Towards Flower Cultivation Technology*

Attitude of the respondents towards flower cultivation technology was ascertained under following subsections:

1. *Pre and Post Exposure Attitude Level*

Table 8 illustrated that 40.11 per cent respondents had unfavourable attitude and nearly same i.e. 37.50 respondents had favourable attitude towards flowers cultivation technology followed by 22.50 percent respondents who had strongly favourable attitude at pre-exposure stage. But after training, majority (62.50%) of the respondents had swing towards strongly favourable attitude followed by favourable (33.75%) and unfavourable (3.75%) towards flower cultivation technology.

Data vividly indicated that 60.00 per cent respondents had favourable attitude towards flower cultivation technology at pre-exposure

TABLE 8

Attitude Level Towards Flower Cultivation Technology

Sr.	*Categories*	*Pre-exposure attitude level*				*Total*	*Post-exposure attitude level*				*Total*
		Jahri n=20	*Garh n=20*	*Sithana n=20*	*Ram Nagar n=20*	*N = 80*	*Jahri n=20*	*Garh n=20*	*Sithana n=20*	*Ram Nagar n=20*	*N = 80*
1.	Unfavourable (15-27)	5(25)	4(20)	6(30)	17(85)	32(40.11)	0(0)	0(0)	0(0)	3(15)	3(3.75)
2.	Favourable (28-39)	5(25)	10(50)	12(60)	3(15)	30(37.50)	5(25)	4(20)	4(20)	14(70)	27(33.75)
3.	Strongly favourable (40-51)	10(50)	6 (30)	2(10)	0(0)	18(22.50)	15(75)	16(80)	16(80)	3(15)	50(62.50)

Figures in parentheses indicate percentages

stage. This is probably so because these rural women belonged to 'self help group' formed under WAMA (Women Awareness and Management Agency) in which groups were formed of those women who's family land is less, low income group and those who are economically motivated, innovation proneness and having risk bearing capacity. Training further proved effective in creating more favorableness towards flower cultivation technology. Similar results has been obtained by Anita (2000) while studying mushroom cultivation technology as she found that respondents were convinced for the adoption of this technology under 'women in agriculture' scheme.

TABLE 9

Attitude Change Index

S.	*Categories*	*Village-wise respondents*				*Total (n=80)*
		Jahri (n=20)	*Garh (n=20)*	*Sithana (n=20)*	*Ram Nagar (n=20)*	
1.	Low (3.92-20.20)	13(65)	9(45)	8(40	11(55)	41(51.25)
2.	Medium (21.26-36.60)	7(35)	8(40)	10(50)	9(45)	34(42.50)
3.	High (37.60-52.94)	0(0)	3(15)	2(10)	0(0)	5(6.25)

Figures in parentheses indicate percentage.

2. Attitude Change Index

Attitude change index calculated with the help of formula explained in the methodology and results are presented in Table 10. It is clear from the data that 51.25 per cent respondents fell under the category of low attitude change index score followed by medium (42.50%). Only 6.25 per cent respondents belonged to high attitude change index category (Table 9).

It seems from the results that more than half of the respondents had low attitude change index score. This may be due to the fact that rural women were already convinced about profitability (feasibility) of the floriculture enterprise.

4. Decision about Adoption of Flower Cultivation

Decision is one of the components of acceptability of flower cultivation technology. Decision refers to mental readiness of the respondents to adopt floriculture technology. Decision to adopt the technology could be different in selected villages. The analysis have been done statement wise as well as attribute wise separately in each of the selected villages and the results have been discussed under following sub-heads:

1. Decision about Adoption of the Technology

Multiple responses were taken to know the decision about adoption of the technology. The respondents on the decision making inventory were asked to reply on each statement under dichotomous response category, i.e. 'yes' or 'no'.

A critical glance at Table 10 reflects that more than half of the respondents (52.50%) were found to be more confident in accepting floriculture due to know-how received through training and were of the opinion that no one can stop them to implement it. Similar percentage of respondents who found it an easy technology inspite of requiring certain precautions. Results further revealed that 52.50 per cent were ready to implement this technology for improving their economic status and 41.25% respondents were fully convinced about the importance of floriculture. The respondent percentage was 33.75 who were ready to implement when 25 per cent of trainees will have already cultivated this technology.

Harvesting and packing of flower is easy task, it was told by 30.00 percent respondents and 43.75 per cent said if they could get good quality saplings, they will implement this technology. Only 5 per cent respondents said that this technology is difficult to understand and have more problems than benefits (3.75%). Being a lady, if is very difficult to procure loan and therefore not ready to implement (5.00%).

TABLE 10

Decision about Implementation of Flower Cultivation Technology

Sr. No.	*Statements*	*Jahri* n=20	*Garh* n=20	*Sithana* n=20	*Ram Nagar* n=20	*Total* N = 80
1.	Being received know how of flower cultivation, I can implement it without hesitation.	14(70)	13(65)	13(65)	2(10)	42(52.50)
2.	The cultivation of flowers, though require certain precautions even then they are easy to follow and can be cultivated without any difficulty	14(70)	13(65)	13(65)	2(10)	42(52.50)
3.	Inspite of social inhibition, I will go for floriculture	10(50)	0(0)	9(45)	0(0)	29(36.25)
4.	The harvesting packing and marketing of flowers is so easy that I can conveniently do it without any problem.	8(40)	7(35)	7(35)	2(10)	24(30.00)
5.	I feel more confident in accepting floriculture due to know how received through training	12(60)	12(60)	10(50)	2(10)	36(45.00)
6.	For improving economic status of family, I will implement it.	15(75)	13(65)	12(60)	2(10)	42(52.50)
7.	As I am fully convinced about the importance of floriculture, no one can stop me to implement it.	10(50)	10(50)	13(65)	0(0)	33(41.25)
8.	I will implement it when 25 % of trainees have cultivated it.	5(25)	7(35)	7(35)	8(40)	27(33.75)

9.	I will implement it only when 25-50 % of the trainees have cultivated it.	0(0)	0(0)	0(0)	6(30)	6(7.50)
10.	I will implement it only when all the trainees have implemented it.	0(0)	0(0)	0(0)	4(20)	4(5.00)
11.	I do not care for others that whether they implement or not but I will never implement it.	0(0)	0(0)	0(0)	0(0)	0(0.00)
12.	If I could get the good quality sapling/ seed at reasonable rate I will implement it.	14(70)	12(60)	7(35)	2(10)	35(43.75)
13.	Inspite of being fully convinced about the importance of flowers, I am not ready to implement.	8(40)	9(45)	0(0)	14(70)	31(38.75)
14.	The cultivation of flowers require more understanding which is beyond to my means and therefore I am not ready to implement.	0(0)	0(0)	0(0)	4(20)	4(5.00)
15.	From training it seems that the cultivation of flowers will have more problems than benefits, so I will not implement it.	0(0)	0(0)	0(0)	3(15)	3(3.75)
16.	Being a lady, it is very difficult to procure loan and without loan, I will not implement it.	0(0)	0(0)	0(0)	4(20)	4(5.00)

Figures in parentheses indicate percentages.

Thus, results lead to conclusion that more than half (52.50%) of the respondents made up their mind to adopt the flower cultivation technology for income generation.

2. Adoption Feasibility of the Technology

Adoption feasibility of floriculture was assessed in terms of certain attributes of the technology like: relative advantage (profitability), cultural compatibility, situational compatibility, simplicity-complexity and tri-ability. Results of the entire four villages have been presented as follows:

1. Adoption Feasibility of Floriculture Technology in Jahri Village

Data presented in Table 11 revealed that maximum number of the respondents of Jahri village perceived this technology as cultural compatibility (mean score 4.55, Ist rank), situational compatible (mean score 4.40, IInd rank), easy to try at small scale (mean score 4.35, IIIrd rank) and similar as relative advantage/profitable. Simple to adopt having mean score 4.1 was ranked fourth. Overall feasibility was found to be 4.35/5.00 (87.00%).

In conclusion cultural, situational compatibility followed by relative advantage contributed in the decision of the technology to adopt.

2. Adoption Feasibility of the Technology in Garh Village

A perusal of data in Table 12 indicated that most of the respondents of Garh village perceived situational compatibility with highest mean score 4.80, ranked Ist followed by profitability of the technology (mean score 4.60, IInd rank), cultural compatibility (mean score 4.50, IIIrd), easy to try (4.25, IVth rank), and simple to adopt (4.00, Vth rank) on small scale before final decision to adopt it. The overall feasibility mean score was 4.43/5.00 (88.60%).

Thus, it can be concluded that situational compatibility and profitability of the technology were the main attributes,

TABLE 11

Adoption Feasibility of Flower Cultivation Technology in Jahri Village (Sonepat)

N = 20

S. No.	*Attributes*	*Feasibility extent*					*Total*	*Mean score*	*Rank*
1.	Relative advantage	Most profitable	Moderately profitable	Somewhat profitable	Least profitable	Not at all profitable			
		12(60)	3(15)	5(25)	0(0)	0(0)	20(100)	4.35	III
2.	Cultural compatibility	Most Suitable	Moderately Suitable	Somewhat Suitable	Least Suitable	Not at all Suitable			
		13(65)	5(25)	2(10)	0(0)	0(0)	20(100)	4.55	I
3.	Situational compatibility	Most Suitable	Moderately Suitable	Somewhat Suitable	Least Suitable	Not at all Suitable			
		11(55)	6(30)	3(15)	0(0)	0(0)	20(100)	4.40	II
4.	Simplicity complexity	Very Simple	Moderately Simple	Niether Simple nor Complex	Moderately Simple	Very Simple			
		8(40	6(30)	6(30)	0(0)	0(0)	20(100)	4.1	IV
5.	Triability	Most Triable	Moderately Triable	Somewhat Triable	Least Triable	Not at all Triable			
		10(50)	7(35)	3(15)	0(0)	0(0)	20(100)	4.35	III

Overall adoption feasibility – 4.35

Figures in parentheses indicate percentages.

TABLE 12

**Adoption Feasibility of Flower Cultivation Technology in Garh Village (Sonepat) **

N = 20

S. No.	Attributes	Feasibility extent					Total	Mean score	Rank
1.	Relative advantage	Most profitable	Moderately profitable	Somewhat profitable	Least profitable	Not at all profitable			
		14(70)	4(20)	2(10)	0(0)	0(0)	20(100)	4.60	II
2.	Cultural compatibility	Most Suitable	Moderately Suitable	Somewhat Suitable	Least Suitable	Not at all Suitable			
		12(60)	6(30)	2(10)	0(0)	0(0)	20(100)	4.5	III
3.	Situational compatibility	Most Suitable	Moderately Suitable	Somewhat Suitable	Least Suitable	Not at all Suitable			
		13(65)	4(20)	3(15)	0(0)	0(0)	20(100)	4.8	I
4.	Simplicity complexity	Very Simple	Moderately Simple	Neither Simple nor complex	Moderately complex	Very Simple			
		7(35)	6(30)	7(35)	0(0)	0(0)	20(100)	4.0	V
5.	Triability	Most Triable	Moderately Triable	Somewhat Triable	Least Triable	Not at all Triable			
		9(45)	7(35)	4(20)	0(0)	0(0)	20(100)	4.25	IV

Overall adoption feasibility – 4.43

Figures in parentheses indicate percentages.

TABLE 13

Adoption Feasibility of Flower Cultivation Technology in Sithana Village (Panipat)

N = 20

S. No.	Attributes	Feasibility extent					Total	Mean score	Rank
1.	Relative advantage	Most profitable	Moderately profitable	Somewhat profitable	Least profitable	Not at all profitable			
		11(55)	5(25)	4(20)	0(0)	0(0)	20(100)	4.35	II
2.	Cultural compatibility	Most Suitable	Moderately Suitable	Somewhat Suitable	Least Suitable	Not at all Suitable			
		12(60)	6(30)	2(10)	0(0)	0(0)	20(100)	4.5	I
3.	Situational compatibility	Suitable Most	Suitable Moderately	Suitable Somewhat	Suitable Least	Suitable Not at all			
		9(45)	4(20)	7(35)	0(0)	0(0)	20(100)	4.1	IV
4.	Simplicity complexity	Very Simple	Moderately Simple	Neither Simple nor complex	Moderately complex	Very Simple			
		9(45)	7(35)	4(20)	0(0)	0(0)	20(100)	4.25	III
5.	Triability	Most Triable	Moderately Triable	Somewhat Triable	Least Triable	Not at all Triable			
		8(40)	5(25)	7(35)	0(0)	0(0)	20(100)	4.05	V

Overall adoption feasibility – 4.25

Figures in parentheses indicate percentages.

which play a significant role in adoption of the technology.

3. Adoption Feasibility of Flower Cultivation Technology in Sithana Village

The Table 13 exhibited the adoption feasibility of the technology in Sithana village. It is noted that overall mean score secured by the respondents was 4.25/5.00 (85.00%). Thus this village ranked IIIrd among all four villages. Data further revealed that cultural compatibility had Ist rank having mean score 4.50 followed by relative advantage (mean score 4.35, IInd rank), simple to adopt (4.25, IIIrd rank), situational compatible (4.1 and IVth rank) and easy to try (4.05, Vth rank) at small scale.

Conclusively, this village respondent also showed Ist preference to cultural compatibility followed by profitability of the technology as main factors to encourage the respondents for adoption. In this village nearly all women were illiterate, so cultural factor played a major role to adopt this technology.

4. Adoption Feasibility of Flower Cultivation Technology in Ram Nagar Village

The adoption feasibility of floriculture technology as depicted in Table 14 emphasized that situational compatibility attribute ranked Ist having mean score 4.00 followed by equally relative advantage and cultural compatibility (mean score 3.15 and ranked IInd), triability (3.00, IIIrd) and easy to follow (2.70, IVth rank) were ranked last.

The overall adoption feasibility was observed as 3.20/5.00 (64.00%). It may be due to illiteracy of all women and low-income group. The village was also not well linked with road transport and cultural factors played a major role inspite of shortage of money.

5. Over All Adoption Feasibility of Flower Cultivation Technology

Analysis of adoption feasibility was done is Table 15 in

TABLE 14

Adoption Feasibility of Flower Cultivation Technology in Ram Nagar Village (Panipat)

N = 20

S. No.	*Attributes*	*Feasibility extent*					*Total*	*Mean score*	*Rank*
1.	Relative advantage	Most profitable	Moderately profitable	Somewhat profitable	Least profitable	Not at all profitable			
		2(10)	6(30)	7(35)	3(15)	2(10)	20(100)	3.15	II
2.	Cultural compatibility	Most Suitable	Moderately Suitable	Somewhat Suitable	Least Suitable	Not at all Suitable			
		2(10)	4(20)	10(50)	3(15)	1(5)	20(100)	3.15	II
3.	Situational compatibility	Most Suitable	Moderately Suitable	Somewhat Suitable	Least Suitable	Not at all Suitable			
		8(40)	6(30)	4(20)	2(10)	0(0)	20(100)	4.00	I
4.	Simplicity complexity	Very Simple	Moderately Simple	Neither Simp- nor complex	Moderately complex	Very Simple			
		2(10)	3(15)	6(30)	5(25)	4(20)	20(100)	2.70	IV
5.	Triability	Most Triable	Moderately Triable	Somewhat Triable	Least Triable	Not at all Triable			
		4(20)	2(10)	6(30)	6(30)	6(30)	20(100)	3.00	III

Overall adoption feasibility – 3.2

Figures in parentheses indicate percentages.

TABLE 15

Over All Adoption Feasibility of Flower Cultivation Technology

N = 80

Sl. No.	*Attributes*	*Village – Wise*				*Attribute wise*	*Rank*
		Jahri (MS)	*Garh (MS)*	*Sithana (MS)*	*Ram Nagar (MS)*	*adoption feasibility (MS)*	
1.	Relative advantage	4.35	4.60	4.35	3.15	4.11	III
2.	Cultural compatibility	4.55	4.50	4.50	3.15	4.18	II
3.	Situational compatibility	4.4	4.80	4.10	4.00	4.33	I
4.	Simplicity complexity	4.1	4.00	4.25	2.70	3.76	V
5.	Triability	4.35	4.25	4.05	3.00	3.91	IV
	Village wise adoption feasibility	4.35	4.43	4.25	3.2	-	-

Over all adoption Feasibility – 4.06

* M.S. = Mean Score

which figures shows that situational compatibility attribute (means score 4.33) followed by cultural compatibility (mean score 4.18) and profitability (mean score 4.11) were major attributes to decide a technology to adopt or reject. Data further revealed that among villages, Garh scored highest mean score (4.43) followed by Jahri (4.35), Sithana (4.25) and Ram Nagar (3.2). The over all adoption feasible villages as well as attribute wise was calculated to 4.06/5.00 (81.20%).

TABLE 16

Adoption Feasibility Index

S. No.	*Categories*	*Village wise respondents*				*Total N = 80*
		Jahri n=20	*Garh n=20*	*Sithana n=20*	*Ram Nagar n=20*	
1.	Low (29.41-52.94)	3(15)	2(10)	3(15)	11(55)	19(23.75)
2.	Medium (53.94-76.47)	3(15)	5(15)	4(20)	7(35)	19(23.75)
3.	High (77.47-100.00)	14(70)	13(65)	13(65)	2(10)	42(52.50)

Figures in parentheses indicate percentages.

The village Garh scored highest mean score because in this village already flower cultivation was done and it is 1-2 km away from Sonepat, which is well linked with rail and road transport. The results of the study further revealed that there is a wide scope to improve the adoption level through modification in attitude and providing facilities like loaning, inputs necessary. As situational, cultural compatibility and relative advantage were the major attributes emerged to made up their mind for final decision to adopt it.

3. Adoption Feasibility Index

Adoption feasibility index for the technology was calculated on the basis of formula explained in the methodology and results (Table 16) exhibit that out of total sample, adoption feasibility was high to 52.50 per cent respondents followed by low and medium (23.75 each) level.

When villages were taken into consideration, it was found that 65 per cent respondents (4.06) in all the villages except in Ram Nagar were ready to adopt this technology inspite of certain problems. In Ram Nagar village, no one wanted to take initiative although two respondents wanted to adopt this technique.

TABLE 17

Implementation of Flower Cultivation Technology

S. No.	*Categories*	*Village wise respondents*				*Total N = 80*
		Jahri n=20	*Garh n=20*	*Sithana n=20*	*Ram Nagar n=20*	
1.	Adopters					
	(a) Adopted imme diately after training	7(35)	8(40)	5(25)	0(0)	24(30.00)
	(b) Adopted after 2-3 visits	3(15)	2(10)	5(25)	0(0)	6(7.50)
2.	Interested adopters	10(50)	10(50)	10(50)	2(10)	32(40.00)
3.	Non-adopters	0(0)	0(0)	0(0)	18(90)	18(22.50)

Figures in parentheses indicate percentages

TABLE 18

Implementation Index

Sl. No.	*Categories*	*Village wise respondents*				*Total N = 80*
		Jahri n=20	*Garh n=20*	*Sithana n=20*	*Ram Nagar n=20*	
1.	Low (1-34)	0(0)	0(0)	0(0)	18(90)	18(22.50)
2.	Medium (35-67)	10(50)	10(50)	10(50)	2(10)	32(40.00)
3.	High (68-100)	10(50)	10(50)	10(50)	0(0)	30(37.50)

Figures in parentheses indicate percentages

Thus, it may be confirmed that adoption feasibility of flower cultivation technology was found to be good for farm women. Only there was need to re-train and motivate them through tested groups, who had already adopted this technology successfully.

5. Implementation Stage

Implementation implies putting an innovation into use on trial basis. Implementation stage was analysed as:

1. Implementation of Flower Cultivation Technology

Data regarding implementation of the technology is presented in table 17. It is clear from the table that irrespective of the villages, among the adopters 30.00 per cent put this practice into use, immediately after training while 7.50 per cent adopted after some persuation (2-3 visits). Fourty per cent respondents were interested in adopting, while 22.50 per cent farm women were non-adopters. The similar interpretation was made by Anita (2000) regarding mushroom production technology where 22.50 per cent respondents put this technology into practice immediately after training while 6.25 per cent respondents tried the technology after some persuation.

Village wise analysis revealed that 50 per cent respondents adopted immediately or after some persuation while 50 per cent respondents were interested but could not adopted this technology because of non availability of raw material at time except in Ram Nagar where only 10 per cent were interested and 90 per cent were non adopters after repeated visits. It was due to their cultural factor which were playing a major role to implement this technology. In addition to this, their illiteracy due to which they did not want to adopt any new thing. It leads to conclusion that at trial stage third forth of the respondents adopted this technology as a result of motivation.

2. Implementation Index

Implementation index was computed with the help of formula explained in methodology and presented in Table 18. It is evident from the results that 50 per cent respondents from each village fall under medium as well as high category of implementation index, respectively except Ram Nagar in which 90 per cent respondents fall under low implementation index followed by 10 per cent in medium category. Irrespective of villages 40 per cent respondent fall under medium category followed by high (37.50%) and low (22.50%) implementation index.

From the above-cited results, it can be inferred that 77.50 per cent farm women had above medium implementation index. It can be said that the respondents of all the villages can be encouraged to accept this technology by providing technical guidance and all necessary requirements.

3. Reasons for Non-adoption of Flowers Cultivation Technology

A critical examination of table 19 indicated that irrespective of villages, hundred per cent respondents said flowers highly perishable nature was the main reason for non-adoption of this technology followed by marketing problem (86%), lack of resources to purchase and availability of required inputs (60%), this practice was not in common use (46%), social bindings and family restriction (42%), complex technology involved and more precaution to be taken care of (40%). Only 10 per cent farm women had health problem and 6 per cent had personal disliking for flowers.

Regarding Jahri village highly perishable nature, non-availability of required material, lack of resources to purchase requisite material and marketing problem were the main reason for non-adoption by 100 per cent respondents. In Garh village reasons for non-adoption as told by 100 per cent respondents were highly perishable nature and small land holding (90%) followed by lack of time and marketing problem (30%).

Highly perishable nature and marketing by (100% respondents each) were the main reasons for non-adoption in Sithana village. While, in Ram Nagar village hundred per cent rural farmwomen told that family restriction, social binding, less profitable crop, highly perishable, complex techniques involved, more precautions to be taken care of, non-availability and lack of resources to purchase required material, not common in use and marketing problem were the reasons for non-adoption of floriculture technology.

TABLE 19

Reasons for Non-Adoption of Flower Cultivation Technology

Sr. No.	*Reasons*	*Jahri n=20*	*Garh n=20*	*Sithana n=20*	*Ram Nagar n=20*	*Total n = 50*
1.	Small land holding	2(20)	9(90)	0(0)	0(0)	11(22)
2.	Lack of time	2(20)	3(30)	0(0)	3(15)	8(16)
3.	Personal disliking	0(0)	0(0)	0(0)	3(15)	3(6)
4.	Family restriction	0(0)	1(10)	0(0)	20(100)	21(42)
5.	Social bindings	0(0)	1(10)	0(0)	20(100)	21(42)
6.	Less profiTable crop	0(0)	0(0)	0(0)	20(100)	20(40)
7.	Highly perishable	10(100)	10(100)	10(100)	20(100)	50(100)
8.	Complex technique involved	0(0)	0(0)	0(0)	20(100)	20(40)
9.	More precautions to be followed	0(0)	0(0)	0(0)	20(100)	20(40)
10.	Less mutual cooperation among women	0(0)	0(0)	0(0)	0(0)	0(0)
11.	Non availability of required material	10(100)	0(0)	0(0)	20(100)	30(60)
12.	Marketing problems	10(100)	3(30)	10(100)	20(100)	43(86)
13.	Not commonly used	0(0)	0(0)	3(30)	20(100)	23(46)
14.	Health problems	0(0)	0(0)	2(20)	3(15)	5(10)
15.	Lack of resources to purchase required material	10(100)	0(0)	0(0)	20(100)	30(60)

Figures in parentheses indicate percentages

Conclusively, it can be said that highly perishable nature of crop, marketing problems, and non-availability or lack of purchasing power were the major reasons for non-adoption of the technology. Accordingly, it can be suggested that special attention should be paid to post harvest management, as nature of crop is highly perishable. In addition to this, a strong marketing network should be established so that more benefit can occur to farmwomen inspite of middlemen. Some incentive can be given to rural women and supply of good quality saplings at reasonable rate will help in more production of good quality flowers on small land and in less time.

4. Constraints Faced by the Respondents in Implementing the Floriculture Technology

Multiple responses were taken to ascertain the constraints faced by the respondents in implementing the technology. Various constraints presented in Table 20 showed that non availability of seeds/sapling (40%), followed by poor quality of seeds/sapling and lack of finance to purchase inputs (26.67%) were the input constraints faced by rural women.

Regarding technical constrains 60 per cent respondents faced difficulty in post harvest management of flowers followed by lack of complete knowledge (43.33%) about different stages of flower production and translocation involved complex procedure.

Quick deterioration of quality of flowers (86.67%), lack of regular market facilities (60%), difficulty in getting good prices of flowers and problems in packing and transportation were marketing constraints faced by farm women.

Majorities of the women (43.33%) were not able to follow complicated procedure for obtaining loan from financial institutions followed by non-availability of government help in the form of credit and subsidy (26.67%), lack of financial assistance (26.67%) and un-assured income from this project

(10%) were the economic constraints. Sindhu and Misra (1997), Singh (2002) and Anita (2002) are reported that lack of technical know-how, not able to follow complicated procedure for obtaining loan from financial institutions, non-availability of quality planting material, infrastructure, unorganized marketing and monitoring system, lacking of sales promotion activities and insufficient cold storage facilities are main constraints in implementation/adoption of this technology.

TABLE 20

Constraints Faced by the Respondents in Implementing the Flower Cultivation Technology

N = 30

Sr. No.	*Constraints*	*Respondents*
1.Input constraints		
—	Non-availability of seeds/saplings	12 (40.00)
—	Poor quality of seeds/saplings	8 (26.67)
—	Low percentage of germination of seeds	0 (0.00)
—	Lack of finance to purchase the inputs	8 (26.67)
—	Environment not favourable for germination of seeds	0 (0.00)
2. Technological constraints		
—	Duration of training not sufficient	0(0.00)
—	Sufficient technical expert are not available	0 (0.00)
—	Translocation involved complex procedure	10 (33.33)
—	Identification of good sapling/seeds is difficult.	0 (0.00)
—	Difficult post harvest management of flowers	18 (60.00)
—	Lack of complete knowledge about different stages of flower production	13 (43.33)
3. Marketing constraints		
—	Lack of regular market facilities	18 (60.00)
—	Problems of packing & transportation	8 (26.67)
—	Difficult to dispose flowers within 2-3 days	0 (0.00)
—	Quick deterioration of the quality of flowers	26 (86.67)
—	Difficulty in getting good prices of flowers	8 (26.67)

4. Economic constraints	
— Lack of financial assistance	8 (26.67)
— Unassured income from this project	3 (10.00)
— Low price of farm produce	0 (0.00)
— Not able to follow complicated procedure for obtaining loan from financial institution	
— Government help in the form of credit and subsidy	8 (26.67)
— Not able to follow complicated procedure for obtaining loan from financial institution	13 (43.33)
5. Physical constraints	
— Body ache due to excessive work	3 (10.00)
— Harmful effect of insecticides, fungicides and weedicides	0 (0.00)

Figures in parentheses indicate percentages.

Physical constraint i.e. body ache due to excessive work was experienced by 10 per cent women.

From this, it can be concluded that quick deterioration of quality flowers, lack of regular market facilities and difficulty in post harvest management of flowers were main constraints faced by majority of the respondents followed by not able to follow complicated procedure for obtaining loan and non-availability of seeds/saplings. Therefore, it can be suggested that problems like post-harvest management should get priority and also sound market facilities. During training women can be trained about loan taking procedures and marketing channels.

5. Cost and Returns of Flower Cultivation Technology

Cost and return analysis was done with the help of three costs

(a) Operational cost: Per acre operational cost included the items like preparatory tillage, pre-sowing irrigation, ridging, seed treatment, sowing, fertilizer application, hoeing, harvesting, packing etc.

(b) Material cost: It includes items such as seed, fertilizer, insecticide pesticides, interest on working capital etc. and,

(c) Fixed cost: It includes items of management and risk charges, transportation charges and rental value of land.

Mandays were calculated for each crop separately and net income calculated including labour charges of family's members and also excluding labour charges of family members. This has been presented under following sections:

1. Mandays Required for Marigold

Total 30 farmwomen i.e. ten from Jahri, and similar from Garh and Sithana village tried the flower cultivation technology under 'self help scheme'. Costs and returns were worked out to estimate net profit obtained from each flower crop each on an acre.

Data from Table 21 indicated that total mandays required for marigold crop were 61.333/acre. Maximum manday's (30.00) were required for hoeing/weeding followed by irrigation and harvesting/picking (7.50 each) and transportation (5.625).

It can be suggested that mandays for hoeing/weeding can be reduced by spraying herbicides.

2. Costs and Returns from Marigold

Costs and return of marigold on an acre has been shown in table 22. Operational cost per acre was found Rs. 4,120/-, which accounted 20.72 per cent of the total costs of Rs. 19,880.88. Among the total operational cost, hoeing/weeding had the major share of Rs. 1,500/- (7.55%), followed by harvesting Rs. 900/- (4.53%) and pre-paratory tillage charges Rs. 800/- (4.02%) of the total cost. Similarly, per acre material cost was observed Rs. 5,197.40, which accounted for 26.14 per cent of the total cost. Irrigation was major item in material cost which accounted for Rs. 1800 per acre and 9.05 per cent of total cost as there was more irrigation needed by marigold crop and water is of tubewell. It was followed by farm yard manure cost Rs.1200/- and 6.04 per cent of total cost and seed i.e. of Rs. 1,000/- per acre accounted 5.03 per cent of total cost.

TABLE 21

Manday's Required for Cultivation of Marigold

	Marigold	
Items		*Manday's/acre*
1.	Preparatory tillage + levelling	1.625
2.	Pre sowing irrigation	0.750
3.	Sowing	0.250
4.	Ridging	2.000
5.	Transplanting	4.000
6.	Seed treatment	—
7.	Manuring	2.000
8.	Fertilizer application	0.083
9.	Irrigation	7.500
10.	Hoeing/weeding	30.000
11.	Plant protection	0.000
12.	Harvesting/picking	7.500
13.	Packing	—
14.	Transportation	5.625
15.	Miscellaneous	—
	Total	61.333

Rental value of land had the major component of Rs. 6,000/- per acre for 6 months, which was 30.18 per cent of total cost followed by transportation of 13.58 per cent of total cost, of Rs. 2700/-. Fixed cost was found to be Rs. 10,563.48.

The main production was observed to be 50 qtl per acre

with the value of Rs. 32,000/-. The per acre returns for marigold cultivation were Rs. 12,119.12 after deducting total cost of Rs. 19,880.88 from the gross return Rs. 32,000 per acre. Income/kg was Rs. 2.42 and per person was Rs. 1,211.19. (At rate of Rs. 80/person, labour charges were of Rs. 4906.64, if family members do work themselves then, benefit could be increased in lieu of labour charges).

TABLE 22

Costs and Returns from Marigold

Year: 2002-03 (Rs./acre)

S. No.	*Particulars*	*Quantity*	*Value*	*Total cost (%)*
I	**Operational cost**			
1.	Preparatory tillage	4	800	4.024
2.	Levelling	1	100	0.503
3.	Pre-sowing irrigation	1	180	0.905
4.	Ridging	1	160	0.805
5.	Seed treatment	-	-	-
6.	Sowing	1	80	0.402
7.	Transplanting	1	320	1.610
8.	Hoeing/weeding	3	1500	7.545
9.	Fertilizer application	2	80	0.402
10.	Harvesting	11.3	900	4.527
11.	Packing	-	-	-
	Sub Total		4,120	20.723
II	**Material cost**			
1.	Seed	400 gm	1000	5.030
2.	Fertilizer nutrients			
	(a). N.	32.0 kg	320.00	1.610
	(b). P	23.0 kg	350.00	1.761
	(c). K.	-	-	-
	(d). Zn	-	-	-
3.	FYM	150 qtl.	1200	6.036
4.	Plant protection	-	-	-

5.	Irrigation	10	1800	9.054
6.	Interest @ 12%	6 months	527.40	2.653
	Sub total		5197.40	26.143
	Total working cost (I+II)		9317.40	46.866
III		**Fixed cost**		
1.	Risk factor		931.74	4.687
2.	Management charges		931.74	4.687
3.	Transportation		2700.00	13.581
4.	Rental value of land	6 months	6000.00	30.180
	Sub total		10563.48	53.134
	Total cost (I+II+III)		19880.88	
	Production:			
	Gross return	5000 kg @ Rs. 6.4/kg	32000.00	
	Return over variable cost		18119.12	
	Net income		12119.12	
	Income/kg		2.42	
	Income/person	10	1211.91	

Average labour charges = Rs. 80 per day
Total labour charges = Rs. 4906.64

It is evident from the results that more income can be obtained in less time and land than other crop (traditional crop).

3. Manday's Required for Gladiolus

On the perusal of data in table 23, it is evident that out of total manday's (89.38), the major share (30.00 manday's) was of hoeing/weeding followed by sowing (20 manday's), transportation (15.00 manday's) and harvesting/picking (7.5 manday's). Conclusively, it can be said that hoeing/weeding were main operation which require maximum manday's. In sowing plot wise cultivation was done at an interval of time so that flowering of all plants do not occur at a point of time. Due to national market of flower in Delhi and perishable nature of flower, they have to be taken on separate vehicle either on fair or own but cannot be taken in local vehicles.

4. Cost and Returns from Gladiolus

Item wise cost of cultivation of gladiolus has been shown in table 24. The total operational cost incurred on different operations in the cultivation of gladiolus was Rs. 6690 per acre, which accounted for 7.60 per cent of total cost Rs. 88,005.20. The major cost items in operations of gladiolus was hoeing/weeding (2.73%) followed by pre-paratory tillage and harvesting (1.48%).

TABLE 23

Manday's Required for Cultivation of Gladiolus

		Gladiolus
Items		Manday's/acre
1.	Preparatory tillage + levelling	1.625
2.	Pre sowing irrigation	—
3.	Sowing	20.000
4.	Ridging	2.000
5.	Transplanting	—
6.	Seed Treatment	0.250
7.	Manuring	6.000
8.	Fertilizer application	0.125
9.	Irrigation	5.625
10.	Hoeing/weeding	30.000
11.	Plant protection	1.250
12.	Harvesting/picking	7.500
13.	Packing	—
14.	Transportation	15.000
15.	Miscellaneous	—
	Total	89.375

Rs. 71,550.40 per acre incurred on different material cost used for cultivation of gladiolus, which was 81.28 per cent of total cost. Cost of seed/bulb was the highest constituent, which was of Rs. 60,000/- accounts for 68.16 per cents of total cost.

TABLE 24

Costs and Returns from Gladiolus

Year: 2002-03 (Rs./acre)

Sr. No.	*Particulars*	*Quantity*	*Value*	*Total cost (%)*
I	**Operational cost**			
1.	Pre-paratory tillage + levelling	6+1	1300	1.477
2.	Pre-sowing irrigation	-	-	-
3.	Ridging	1	160	0.182
4.	Seed treatment	1	300	0.341
5.	Sowing	1	1200	1.363
6.	Fertilizer application	3	30	0.034
7.	Hoeing/weeding	4	2400	2.727
8.	Harvesting	1	1300	1.477
9.	Packing	-	-	-
	Sub Total		6690	7.600
II	**Material cost**			
1.	Seed	60000 bulb	60,000	68.161
2.	Fertilizer nutrients			
	(a). N.	44.5 kg	471.7	0.536
	(b). P	23.0 kg	350	0.400
	(c). K	-	-	-
	(d). Zn	-	-	-
3.	FYM	280 qtl.	2240	2.545
4.	Plant protection	10	1300	1.477
5.	Irrigation	15	2700	3.067
6.	Interest @ 12% for half of growth period	6 month	4488.70	5.099
	Sub total		71550.40	81.283
	Total working cost (I+II)		78240.40	88.883

III	Fixed cost			
1.	Risk factor		782.40	0.901
2.	Management charges		782.40	0.901
3.	Transportation		3200	3.635
4.	Rental value of land	6 month	5000	5.680
	Sub total		9,764.80	11.117
	Total cost (I+II+III)		88005.20	
	Production			
	Gross return (Rs.)		1,59,000	
	Return over variable cost		75,994.80	
	Net return (income)		70,994.80	
	Income/stick		1.69	
	Income/person	10	7099.48	

Average labour charges = Rs. 80/day
Total labour charge = Rs. 7150

Fixed cost calculated as Rs. 9,764.80 per acre accounts for 11.12 per cent total cost i.e. Rs. 88,005.20, among which transportation (Rs. 3,200/-, 3.64%) and rental value of land (5000/-, 5.68%) were the major components.

All the three total cost of cultivation of gladiolus was calculated Rs. 88,005.20 per acre. In cultivation of gladiolus, material cost was highest with 81.28 per cent of total cost. Net return of Rs. 70,994.80 per acre obtained from the gladiolus cultivation after deducting total cost from the gross return, which was Rs. 1,59,000/- per acre. On an average, income per person obtained as Rs. 7099.48 per acre. Labour charges of family members were Rs. 7150.

5. Manday's Required for Cultivation of Chrysanthemum

Table 25 showed that out of total manday's (64.08) required for chrysanthemum cultivation, 30 manday's were necessary for hoeing/weeding followed by irrigation (9 manday's), harvesting/picking (7.5 manday's) and transplantation (5 manday's).

Like marigold, chrysanthemum required maximum manday's for hoeing/weeding and irrigation.

6. Costs and Returns from Chrysanthemum

Item wise costs of cultivation of chrysanthemum are shown in Table 26. Cost incurred on different operations in chrysanthemum cultivation was Rs. 4,400/- per acre, which accounted for 22.30 per cent. Main cost items in operations of chrysanthemum were hoeing/weeding of Rs. 1,500/- accounted for 7.60 per cent followed by pre-paratory tillage (5.07%) of Rs. 1,000/- and harvesting (Rs. 900/- and 4.56%).

TABLE 25

Manday's Required for Cultivation of Chrysanthemum

		Chrysanthemum
Items		*Manday's/acre*
1.	Preparatory tillage + levelling	1.875
2.	Pre sowing irrigation	0.750
3.	Sowing	0.250
4.	Ridging	2.000
5.	Transplanting	5.000
6.	Seed treatment	—
7.	Manuring	2.000
8.	Fertilizer application	0.083
9.	Irrigation	9.000
10.	Hoeing/weeding	30.000
11.	Plant protection	0.000
12.	Harvesting/picking	7.500
13.	Packing	—
14.	Transportation	5.625
15.	Miscellaneous	—
	Total	64.083

Rs. 4790.20/- per acre incurred on different materials used for chrysanthemum cultivation, which was 24.28 per cent of total cost. Cost of irrigation (Rs. 1800) was highest accounts for 9.12 per cent followed by cost of farm yard manure Rs. 1200 (6.08%).

TABLE 26

Costs and Returns from Chrysanthemum

Year: 2002-03 (Rs./acre)

Sr. No.	*Particulars*	*Quantity*	*Value*	*Total cost (%)*
I	**Operational cost**			
1.	Pre-paratory tillage	5	1000	5.069
2.	Levelling	1	100	0.507
3.	Pre-sowing irrigation	1	180	0.912
4.	Ridging	1	160	0.811
5.	Seed treatment	—	—	—
6.	Sowing	1	80	0.406
7.	Transplanting	1	400	2.028
8.	Hoeing/weeding	3	1500	7.603
9.	Fertilizer application	—	80	0.406
10.	Harvesting	11.3	900	4.562
11.	Packing	—	—	—
	Sub total		4400	22.303
II	**Material cost**			
1.	Seed	150 gm	600	3.041
2.	Fertilizer nutrients			
	(a) N.	32.0 kg	320.00	1.622
	(b) P	23.0 kg	350.00	1.774
	(c) K.	—	—	—
	(d) Zn	—	—	—
3.	FYM	150 qtl.	1200	6.083
4.	Plant protection	—	—	—
5.	Irrigation	10	1800	9.124
6.	Interest @ 12%	6 months	520.20	2.637
	Sub total		4790.20	24.281
	Total working cost (I+II)		9190.20	46.584

III		**Fixed cost**		
1.	Risk factor		919.02	4.658
2.	Management charges		919.02	4.658
3.	Transportation		2700.00	13.686
4.	Rental value of land	6 months	6000.00	30.413
	Sub total		10538.04	53.416
	Total cost (I+II+III)		19728.24	
	Production:			
	Gross return	5500 kg @		
		Rs. 7/kg	38500.00	
	Return over variable cost		24771.76	
	Net return		18771.76	
	Income/kg		3.41	
	Income/person	10 women	1877.76	

Average labour charges = Rs. 80/day

Total labour charge = Rs. 5126.64

Fixed cost calculated as Rs. 10538.04 per acre among, which rental value of land Rs. 6000/- accounts for 30.41 per cent of total cost. Rs. 19728.24 was calculated as total cost of cultivation of chrysanthemum. Net returns of Rs. 18,771.76 per acre were obtained after deducting total cost from the gross returns which was Rs. 38,500/-. Net income/kg came out to be Rs. 3.41 and income per person was Rs. 1877.76. Labour charges involved in chrysanthemum on one acre were Rs. 5126.64.

Net return is little more than marigold although cost of cultivation was nearly same.

7. Manday's Required for Cultivation of Rose

Data from table 27 revealed that 40 manday's were required in sowing as well as hoeing/weeding operations, followed by transportation (33.75% manday's), harvesting/picking (11.25 manday's) and manuring (10 manday's). Total manday's required for rose cultivation were 141.83.

Results of the table showed that rose cultivation required maximum manday's from all other four crops. But it is a perennial crop, once cultivated, remains for 4-5 years and gives yield.

8. Costs and Returns from Rose Cultivation

Harvesting/picking of Rs. 6,000 accounts for 14.08 per cent of total cost of rose cultivation followed by cost of hoeing/weeding Rs. 3200 (7.51%). Total operation cost of rose cultivation was Rs 10,650/- accounts for 24.99 per cent of total cost of rose cultivation.

TABLE 27

Manday's Required for Cultivation of Rose

		Rose
Items		*Manday's/acre*
1.	Preparatory tillage + levelling	0.375
2.	Pre sowing irrigation	—
3.	Sowing	40.000
4.	Ridging	1.000
5.	Transplanting	—
6.	Seed treatment	—
7.	Manuring	10.000
8.	Fertilizer application	0.208
9.	Irrigation	4.500
10.	Hoeing/weeding	40.000
11.	Plant protection	0.750
12.	Harvesting/picking	11.250
13.	Packing	—
14.	Transportation	33.750
15.	Miscellaneous	—
	Total	141.833

Table 28 further revealed that from material cost (Rs. 11,880) seeds/ seedling accounts for 9.39 per cent of total cost Rs. 42,611 per acre of rose cultivation. Material cost accounts for 27.88 per cent of total cost of cultivation/acre.

TABLE 28

Costs and Returns from Rose

Year: 2002-03 (Rs./acre)

Sr. No.	*Particulars*	*Quantity*	*Value*	*Total cost (%)*
I	**Operational cost**			
1.	Pre-paratory tillage + levelling	1	300	0.704
2.	Pre-sowing irrigation	—	—	—
3.	Ridging	1	100	0.235
4.	Seed treatment	—	—	—
5.	Sowing	1	1000	2.347
6.	Fertilizer application	4	50	0.117
7.	Hoeing/weeding		3200	7.510
8.	Harvesting/picking		6000	14.081
9.	Packing		—	—
	Sub Total		10650	24.994
II	**Material cost**			
1.	Seed or seedling		7000	9.387
2.	Fertilizer nutrients			
	(a) N.	21.5 kg	227.90	0.535
	(b) P	31.0 kg	507.07	1.190
	(c) K	30.0 kg	215.00	0.505
	(d) Zn	21.1 kg	300.00	0.704
3.	FYM			
4.	Plant protection	3	880.00	2.065
5.	Irrigation		720.00	1.690
6.	Interest @ 12%	6 months	2030.00	4.764
	Sub total		11880.00	27.880
	Total working cost (I+II)		22530.00	52.874

III		Fixed cost		
1.	Risk factor		2253.00	5.287
2.	Management charges		2253.00	5.287
3.	Transportation		5575.00	13.084
4.	Rental value of land	6 months	10000.00	23.468
	Sub total		20081.00	47.126
	Total cost (I+II+III)		42611.00	
	Production			
	Gross return	8000 kg @	80000.00	
	Return/income over variable cost	Rs. 10/kg	43389.00	
	Net income		37389.00	
	Income/kg		10.85	
	Income/person		3738.90	

Average labour charges = Rs. 80/day

Total labour charge = Rs. 11346.64

From fixed cost of Rs. 20,081 (47% of total cost of cultivation of rose/acre) rental value of land was Rs. 10,000 accounts for maximum cost i.e. 23.47 per cent followed by transportation of Rs. 5,575 (13.08%). Gross return came out to be Rs. 80,000 per acre while total cost of cultivation of rose on one acre was Rs. 42,611. Thus, net return of Rs. 37,389 obtained and income/ person as Rs. 3738.90. Labour charges of family members were highest in rose cultivation i.e. Rs. 11346.64 in the first season of cultivation.

Conclusively, the results exhibited that in rose cultivation maximum cost was of rental value of land and labour charges. It is a prelinear crop, benefits will be obtained for 3-4 years after this investment. Returns over years cannot be calculated due to limitations of research period and this return is a lower limit of the crop.

9. Manday Required for Tuberose Cultivation

Table 29 showed that transportation of tuberose required maximum manday's i.e. 22.50 followed by sowing (20), hoeing/

weeding and harvesting/picking (15 each). Total manday's required for cultivation of tuberose were 86.42.

As maximum manday required for transport because it is very perishable flower so regular (daily) sale of it to national market at Delhi, for getting good price is necessary. Regarding sowing, plot wise sowing at an interval of time is necessary so that all plants do not flower at a time rather after an interval.

10. Costs and Returns from Tuberose

In Table 30 indicated that the operational cost was Rs. 5165 per acre, which accounted 8.63 per cent of the total cost of Rs. 59840.56. Among the total operational cost, harvesting had major share of Rs. 1800 (3.01%), followed by hoeing/weeding plus earthing charges Rs. 1200 (2.01%) of total cost.

TABLE 29

Manday Required for Cultivation of Tuberose

		Tuberose
Items		*Manday/acre*
1.	Preparatory tillage + levelling	1.500
2.	Pre sowing irrigation	—
3.	Sowing	20.000
4.	Ridging	5.000
5.	Transplanting	—
6.	Seed treatment	0.250
7.	Manuring	5.000
8.	Fertilizer application	0.167
9.	Irrigation	1.500
10.	Hoeing/weeding	15.000
11.	Plant protection	0.375
12.	Harvesting/picking	15.000
13.	Packing	—
14.	Transportation	22.500
15.	Miscellaneous	0.125
	Total	86.417

TABLE 30

Costs and Returns From Tuberose

Year: 2002-03 (Rs./acre)

Sr. No.	*Particulars*	*Quantity*	*Value*	*Total cost (%)*
I	**Operational cost**			
1.	Pre-paratory tillage	4	800	1.337
2.	Levelling	1	100	0.167
3.	Pre-sowing irrigation	—	—	—
4.	Ridging	1	550	0.919
5.	Seed treatment	—	75	0.125
6.	Sowing	1	600	1.002
7.	Fertilizer application	2	40	0.067
8.	Hoeing/weeding + earthing	4	1200	2.005
9.	Harvesting	2	1800	3.008
10.	Packing	—	—	—
	Sub total		5165	8.631
II	**Material cost**			
1.	Seed	64,000 bulb	32000	53.475
2.	Fertilizer nutrients			
	(a). N.	36.0 kg	360.00	0.602
	(b). P	23.0 kg	350.00	0.585
	(c). K.	—	—	—
	(d). Zn	—	—	—
3.	FYM	187.5 qtl.	1500	2.507
4.	Plant protection	1	275	0.460
5.	Irrigation	6	1080	1.805
6.	Interest @ 12%	6 months	2803.80	4.685
	Sub total		38368.80	64.118
	Total working cost (I+II)		43533.80	72.750
III	**Fixed cost**			
1.	Risk factor		4353.38	7.275
2.	Management charges		4353.38	7.275

3.	Transportation		3600.00	6.016
4.	Rental value of land	6 months	4000.00	6.684
	Sub total		16306.76	27.250
	Total cost (I+II+III)		59840.56	
	Production:			
	Gross return		1,26,000	
	Return over variable cost		70,159.44	
	Net return		66,159.44	
	Income/stick		1.58	
	Income /person	10	6615.94	

Average labour charges = Rs. 80/day

Total labour charge = Rs. 6913.36

Material cost was observed to be Rs. 38368.80, which is equivalent to 64.12 per cent of total cost of cultivation in one acre. It includes Rs. 2803.80 as interest on working capital (4.69%) which is the major constituent followed by farm yard manure (2.41%).

In fixed cost, risk factor and management charges were major factor causing maximum cost of Rs. 4353.38 each of total cost (7.28%), followed by rental value of land (6.68%) and transportation (6.02%). Fixed cost accounts for 27.25 per cent of total cost of cultivation of tuberose i.e. Rs. 59840.56.

The per acre net returns for tuberose cultivation Rs. 66,159.44 after deducting the total cost Rs. 59,840.56 from gross return which were of Rs. 1,26,200/-. Income per person came out to be Rs. 6615.94. In total cost Rs. 6913.36 were due to family labour charges.

This lead to the conclusion that per person income/acre was lower than gladiolus.

11. Comparison of Manday Required for Marigold, Gladiolus, Chrysanthemum, Rose and Tuberose

After observing table 31, it can be analysed that maximum

manday were required for rose crop (141.83) followed by gladiolus (89.38) and tuberose (86.42%). All the flower crops required maximum manday in hoeing/weeding except tuberose which required maximum manday's in transportation. Marigold and chrysanthemum required highest manday's (30) in hoeing/weeding, while gladiolus, rose and tuberose required/needed maximum manday in sowing as well as transportation. The results leads to conclusion that this enterprise required more labour than other traditional crops. Chattopadhyay (2000) supported these results & said that due to intensive and specialized type of work, floriculture enterprise engages 8-10 skilled and unskilled workers per hectare throughout the year, in addition to a large number of self employed workers for processing, transportation and marketing.

12. Comparative Costs and Returns from Marigold, Gladiolus Chrysanthemum, Rose and Tuberose.

It was apparent from table 32 that for cultivation of rose, highest operational cost was required, which was 24.99 per cent of total cost of cultivation of Rose i.e. Rs. 42,611/-. Material cost needed for gladiolus was maximum (Rs. 71,550.40; 81.28% of total cost) followed by tuberose (Rs. 38,368.80; 61.65% of total cost). Total working cost of gladiolus was highest i.e. Rs. 78,240.40, whereas fixed cost required for tuberose was maximum. After analysis, it was found that total cost of cultivation of gladiolus was highest i.e. Rs. 88005.20 followed by tuberose (Rs. 59,840.56), Rose (Rs. 42,611.00) marigold (Rs. 19,880.88/-) and chrysanthemum (Rs. 19728.24/-). Income per person was maximum of gladiolus growers i.e. Rs. 7,099.48 followed by rose (Rs. 3,738.90), tuberose (Rs. 3,000.00), chrysanthemum (Rs. 1,877.76) and marigold (Rs. 1,211.91).

TABLE 31

Comparative Manday Required for Cultivation of Marigold, Gladiolus, Chrysanthemum, Rose and Tuberose

Items	*Marigold*	*Cladiolus*	*Chrysan--themum*	*Rose*	*Tuberose*
1. Preparatory tillage + levelling	1.625	1.625	1.875	0.375	1.500
2. Pre sowing irrigation (Tubewell/Canal)	0.750	—	0.750	—	—
3. Sowing	0.250	20.000	0.250	40.000	20.000
4. Ridging	2.000	2.000	2.000	1.000	5.000
5. Transplanting	4.000	—	5.000	—	—
6. Seed treatment	—	0.250	—	—	0.250
7. Manuring	2.000	6.000	2.000	10.000	5.000
8. Fertilizer application	0.083	0.125	0.083	0.208	0.167
9. Irrigation	7.500	5.625	9.000	4.500	1.500
10. Hoeing/weeding	30.000	30.000	30.000	40.000	15.000
11. Plant protection	0.000	1.250	0.000	0.750	0.375
12. Harvesting/picking	7.500	7.500	7.500	11.250	15.000
13. Packing	—	—	—	—	—
14. Transportation	5.625	15.000	5.625	33.750	22.500
15. Miscellaneous	—	—	—	—	0.125
Total	61.333	89.375	64.083	141.833	86.417

Thus it can be concluded that after heavy investment in gladiolus and tuberose, the net returns were also highest. In rose, after medium investment, there will be benefit for 3-4 years continuously after only some expenditure on management. Regarding marigold and chrysanthemum, there was little investment and less benefit in comparison to other flower crops but still these are good than traditional crops.

TABLE 32

Comparative Costs and Returns from Marigold, Gladiolus, Chrysanthemum, Rose and Tuberose

Items	*Marigold*	*Cladiolus*	*Chrysan- -themum*	*Rose*	*Tuberose*
Operational cost (Rs.)	4,120.00 (20.72)	6,690.00 (7.28)	4,400.00 (22.30)	10,650.00 (24.99)	5,165 (8.30)
Materials cost (Rs.)	5,197.40 (26.14)	71,550.40 (81.28)	4,790.20 (24.28)	11,880.00 (27.88)	38,368.80 (61.65)
Working cost (Rs.)	9,317.40 (46.86)	78,240.40 (88.88)	9,190.20 (46.58)	22,530.00 (52.87)	43,533.80 (69.72)
Fixed cost (Rs.)	10,563.48 (53.13)	9,764.80 (11.12)	10,538.04 (53.41)	20,081.00 (47.13)	16,306.76 (27.25)
Total cost (Rs.)	19,880.88	88,005.20	19,728.24	42,611.00	59,840.56
Gross return (Rs.)	32,000.00	1,59,000.00	38,500.00	80,000.00	94840.00
Net return (Rs)	12,119.12	70,994.80	18,771.76	37,389.00	35000.00
Income (Rs)/stick (kg)	2.42	1.69	3.41	10.85	0.73
Income/person (Rs)	1211.91	7,099.48	1,877.76	3,738.90	3500.00
Returns per rupee of investment	60.96%	80.67%	95.15%	87.75%	58.49%
Rank	IV	III	I	II	V

Figures in parenthesis indicate percentages

6. Confirmation Stage

It refers to reinforcement of an innovation decision already made. Confirmation to adopt the flower cultivation technology was ascertained under following sub sections:

1. Adoption of the Technology

The result regarding confirmation about adoptions of floriculture technology are reported in Table 33. Successful results of the implementation stage encourages non-adopters of all the four villages, as at the confirmation stage number of farm women who adopted floriculture became double except in Ram Nagar. All the adopters did experiment their crop in-group.

The results depicts that 87.50 per cent of the respondents adopted this technology out of which 32.50 per cent respondents adopted immediately after completion of first crop while 28.75 per cent adopted after seeing the benefit of first crop whereas, 26.25 per cent adopted after seeing the profit of first crop, in addition to this further motivation. Village wise analysis revealed that in Jahri, Garh and Sithana village, there was 100 per cent adoption whereas in Ram Nagar, there was 50 per cent adoption. The results shows that remaining 13.50 per cent can be easily motivated to adopt the technology, there is need of some motivation or they will adopt after seeing that whole group adopted this technology & found profit because they are the laggards as observed by Das and Mitra (1994) in case of marigold crop.

2. *Adoption/Confirmation Index*

It was observed from Table 34 that majority of respondents (61.25%) fall in high confirmation index followed by medium (26.25%) and low (12.50%).

Village wise evaluation highlighted that among the high adoption category, majority was from Jahri (100%) and Garh village (100%) which indicate their eagerness to adopt flower cultivation technology as an innovation. While in Sithana village 55 per cent farm women fall under medium and 45 per cent in high confirmation index. On the contrary, equal number (50%) of the respondents of Ram Nagar village, had medium as well as low confirmation index.

7. Overall Acceptability of Flower Cultivation Technology

Acceptability index of floriculture technology was analyzed in term of knowledge gain, attitude change, decision to adopt the technology, implementation and confirmation. The encouraging results have been presented in Table 35. It is apparent from the table that out of total sample, 48.75 per cent respondents were observed in medium and 35.00 per cent in high (35%) category of acceptability whereas only 16.25 per cent respondents were found in low category. These results were in contradiction with Dahiya (1999) who observed 67 per cent respondents had low level of adoption of floriculture followed by medium (23%) and only 10 per cent fall under high level of adoption.

Table 33

Confirmation of Flower Cultivation Technology

Sr. No.	*Reasons*	*Village wise respondent*				*Total (n = 80)*
		Jahri (n=20)	*Garh (n=20)*	*Sithana (n=20)*	*Ram Nagar (n=20)*	
1.	Adopted immediately after after completion of first crop	10(50)	10(50)	6(30)	0(0)	26(32.50)
2.	Adopted after seeing profit of crop grown of 1st group	10 (50)	10 (50)	3 (15)	0(0)	23 (28.75)
3.	Seeing the profit + further motivation	0(0)	0(0)	11 (55)	10 (50)	21 (26.25)
4.	Not at all adopted	0(0)	0(0)	0(0)	10 (50)	10 (12.50)

Figures in parentheses indicate percentages

TABLE 34

Confirmation Index

Sr. No.	*Categories*	*Village wise respondent*				*Total (n = 80)*
		Jahri (n=20)	*Garh (n=20)*	*Sithana (n=20)*	*Ram Nagar (n=20)*	
1.	Low (1-34)	0(0)	0(0)	0(0)	10(50)	10(12.50)
2.	Medium (35-67)	0(0)	0(0)	11 (55)	10(50)	21(26.25)
3.	High (68-100)	20 (100)	20 (100)	9(45)	0(0)	49(61.25)

Figures in parentheses indicate percentages

TABLE 35

Over All Acceptability Index of the Flower Cultivation Technology

Sr. No.	*Categories*	*Village wise respondent*				*Total (n = 80)*
		Jahri (n=20)	*Garh (n=20)*	*Sithana (n=20)*	*Ram Nagar (n=20)*	
1.	Low (26.18-32.99)	1(5)	3(15)	0(0)	9(45)	13(16.25)
2.	Medium (33.99-39.80)	10(50)	10(50)	10(50)	9(45)	39(48.75)
3.	High (40.80-46.61)	9(45)	7(35)	10(50)	2(10)	28(35.00)

Figures in parentheses indicate percentages

When villages were taken in to consideration, the results revealed that respondents of Jahri (95%), Garh (85%), Sithana (100%) and Ram Nagar (55 %) villages accepted this technology appropriate for income generation. This clearly indicated that there is a tremendous potential for the production of flowers as an income-generating project. Rural women were very keen to learn the technology in order to enhance their socio-economic status. Majority of women had adopted this technology inspite of their poor education, social pressure and other constraints.

8. *Relationship between Acceptability of Flower Cultivation Technology and Profile Variables*

The results in table 36 exhibited the relationship between acceptability and profile variables. As regards knowledge gain, table revealed that occupation (r = 0.222) had significant positive relationship with knowledge gain. This means that families which already cultivated flowers, the respondents of these families gain more knowledge than non-growers of flowers. Education (r = +0.384) and economic motivation (+0.240) had significant positive relationship with attitude change about flower cultivation technology at five per cent level of significance. As the education increases, attitude change took place and also same with economic motivation.

Family type (r = 0.240), education (r = 0.247), innovation proneness (0.053), risk orientation (r = 0.542), economic motivation (r = 0.517) and market access (r = 0.356) had positive significant correlation with adoption feasibility. It mean that disintegration of joint family system, higher the education, attitude like innovation proneness, risk bearing capacity and economically motivated and nearness of national market forced the person to look for alternate sources of income. Thus psychological and situation factor i.e. market access might have mobilized the rural women to adopt flower cultivation technology.

Socio-economic status (r = 0.238), communication variables (r = 0.375), innovation proneness (r = 0.662), risk orientation (r = 0.547), market access (r = 0.432) had positive significant correlation with implementation of the technology. This shows that higher the status and more communication sources, more was the implementation of the technology. More innovative person having high risk bearing capacity was ready to implement the technology.

Confirmation of the technology was positively correlated with caste, socio-economic status (r = 0.342), innovation proneness (r = 0.760), risk orientation (r = 0.734), economic motivation (r = 0.621) and market access (r = 0.516). In addition to above, caste was additional. This means that higher the caste, more confirmation to adopt the technology.

Similarly acceptability of the technology was found to have positive significant relationship with psychology variables and market access whereas acceptability was negatively correlated with material possession (r = -0.231). It leads to the meaning that more the material possession a person had lesser will be acceptability of the innovation and vice-versa.

Thus, results lead to conclusion that psychological variables i.e. innovation proneness, risk orientation, economic motivation and market access i.e. nearness to market emanated as the main contributory factor to change attitude, decision to adopt, implement, confirm and accept the technology.

9. *Multiple Regression Analysis of Trainees about Flower Cultivation Technology with Significant Independent Variables*

Multiple regression analysis was calculated to know more precisely the variation of significant variables, to what extent significant variables effected trainee's knowledge, attitude, decision, adoption and confirmation.

Multiple regression had been analysed under following sub-sections:

1. *Multiple Regression Analysis of Trainees Knowledge and Attitude about Flower Cultivation Technology with Significant Independent Variables*

Multiple regression analysis presented in table 37 showed that only occupation explained 28.60 per cent variation in knowledge level of the respondents. The 't' value indicated that occupation had insignificant effect on the knowledge level of the respondents. Whereas, education and economic motivation were significant with attitude and variation in attitude was 31.90 per cent with education and economic motivation. Only education had significant effect on attitude. This clearly indicated that change in attitude about flower cultivation technology was due to education, while economic motivation did not affected attitude to a significant level and knowledge was not significantly affected by occupation or any other independent variable.

TABLE 36

Correlation of Profile Variable with Acceptability of Flower Cultivation Technology

Sr. No.	Profile variables	Knowledge gain	Attitude change	Adoption feasibility	Implementation	Confirmation	Acceptability
1.	Age	-0.198	-0.053	-0.013	0.052	0.082	-0.069
2.	Caste	-0.031	-0.038	0.080	0.120	0.270*	0.051
3.	Family type	-0.156	-0.092	0.240*	0.116	0.149	0.135
4.	Family size	-0129	-0.091	0.206	0.219	0.146	0.153
5.	Land holding	0.093	0.098	-0.081	0.073	0.074	0.046
6.	Occupation	0.222*	-0.081	0.135	-0.043	0.020	0.081
7.	Education	-0.022	0.384*	0.247*	0.063	0.107	0.038
8.	Income	-0.026	-0.202	0.020	0.106	0.108	-0.039
9.	Material possession	-0.081	-0.080	-0.168	-0.177	-0.278*	-0.231*
10.	Socio-economic status	0.021	-0.205	0.205	0.238*	0.342*	0.141
11.	Communication variables	0.113	-0.059	-0.139	0.375*	0.450*	-0.184
12.	Innovation proneness	-0.038	-0.154	0.523*	0.662*	0.760*	0.466*
13.	Risk orientation	0.004	-0.154	0.542*	0.663*	0.734*	0.492*
14.	Economic motivation	-0.013	0.240*	0.517*	0.547*	0.621*	0.418*
15.	Cropping pattern	0.165	0.113	-0.147	-0.189	-0.177	-0.050
16.	Farming system	0.104	0.069	-0.005	-0.178	-0.056	0.020
17.	Market access	-0.186	0.071	0.356*	0.432*	0.516*	0.343*

* Significant at 5% level of significance

TABLE 37

Multiple Regression Analysis of Trainees Knowledge and Attitude About Flower Cultivation Technology with Significant Independent Variables

Sl. No.	*Independent variables*	*'b' values*	*'t' values*	*R^2*	*'f' value*
1.	**Knowledge**				
	Occupation	0.037	0.317	0.286	1.359
2	**Attitude**				
	Education	-2.528*	-2.372	0.319	1.590
	Economic motivation	1.253	1.208		

* Significant at 5 per cent level of significance

2. *Multiple Regression Analysis of Trainees Adoption Fealibility Towards Flower Cultivation Technology with Significant Independent Variables*

The multiple regression analysis presented in table 38 showed that the six significant independent variables were taken and these explained 47.70 per cent variation in adoption of the respondents. The 't' value indicated that none of the variable had significant effect on symbolic adoption.

TABLE 38

Multiple Regression Analysis of Trainees Adoption Feasibility about Flower Cultivation Technology with Significant Independent Variables

Sl. No.	*Independent variables*	*'b' values*	*'t' values*	*R^2*	*'f' value'*
1.	Family type	2.813	1.613		
2.	Education	-0.451	-0.542		
3.	Innovation proneness	-0.669	-0.754	0.477	3.088
4.	Risk orientation	1.245	1.692		
5.	Economic motivation	1.028	1.271		
6.	Market access	0.064	-0.127		

* Significant at 5 per cent level of significance

TABLE 39

Multiple Regression Analysis of Trainees Implementation about Flower Cultivation Technology with Significant Independent Variables

Sl. No.	*Independent variables*	*'b' values*	*'t' values*	*R^2*	*'f' value'*
1.	Socio-economic status	0.027	0.493		
2.	Communication variables	0.034	1.327		
3.	Innovation proneness	0.135	-0.822	0.670	6.879
4.	Risk orientation	0.231	1.696		
5.	Economic motivation	0.042*	2.782		
6.	Market access	0.033	0.357		

* Significant at 5 per cent level of significance

3. *Multiple Regression Analysis of Trainees Implementation Towards Flower Cultivation Technology with Significant Independent Variables*

The multiple regression analysis of trainees presented in table 39 revealed that significant independent variables like socio-economic status, communication variables, innovation proneness, risk orientation, economic motivation, market access and situational variables explained 67 per cent variation in implementation of the technology. Out of these variables economic motivation and situational variables were mainly responsible for implementation of the technology. This means that women who wanted to earn money and if situation is suited, they will surely implement this technology.

4. *Multiple Regression Analysis of Trainees Confirmation about Flower Cultivation Technology with Significant Independent Variables*

When the multiple regression co-efficient (R2) was calculated on the data (Table 40), it was found that 78.3 per cent variation in confirmation of the technology by the respondents was explained by 8 independent variables. These variables were caste, material possession, socio-economic status, communication variables, innovation proneness, risk orientation, economic motivation, market access and situational variables. Out of these, eight independent variables, material possession, socio-economic status, communication variables and situational variables were main contributing for the effect on confirmation about flower cultivation.

Thus, it can be concluded that socio-economic and communication variables affected confirmation to positive direction while material possession and situational variables affect it in negative direction.

TABLE 40

Multiple Regression Analysis of Trainees Confirmation about Flower Cultivation Technology with Significant Independent Variables

Sl. No.	*Independent variables*	*'b' values*	*'t' values*	R^2	*'f' value'*
1.	Caste	-0.108	-1.452		
2.	Material possession	-0.022*	-2.705		
3.	Socio-economic status	0.090*	2.127		
4.	Communication variables	0.041*	2.076		
5.	Innovation proneness	0.126	1.006	0.783	12.247
6.	Risk orientation	0.064	0.610		
7.	Economic motivation	0.176	1.540		
8.	Market access	0.062	0.879		

*Significant at 5 per cent level of significance

TABLE 41

Multiple Regression Analysis of Trainees Overall Acceptance about Flower Cultivation Technology with Significant Independent Variables

Sl. No.	*Independent variables*	*'b' values*	*'t' values*	R^2	*'f' value'*
1.	Material possession	-0.059	-1.019		
2.	Innovation proneness	-1.867*	2.074		
3.	Risk orientation	1.820*	2.439	0.466	2.960
4.	Economic motivation	1.932*	2.352		
5.	Market access	0.203	0.397		

* Significant at 5 per cent level of significance

5. Multiple Regression Analysis of Trainees Acceptance about Flower Cultivation with Significant Independent Variables

When the multiple regression co-efficient (R2) was estimated on the data (Table 38), it was found that 46.60 per cent variation in acceptance of the technology of the respondents was explained by five significant independent variables. These variables were material possession, innovation proneness, risk orientation, economic motivation, market access. Out of these variables innovation proneness, risk orientation, economic motivations were mainly responsible for acceptance of the technology. This means that with the increase in all these variables, i.e. a women is innovative, having risk bearing capacity and more eager to earn money, there will be increase in acceptance of the flower cultivation technology.

In conclusion, it can be said that education significantly affected attitude to 31.90 per cent variation. Implementation of flower cultivation technology was affected by economic motivation to the degree of 67 per cent. Confirmation of the technology was significantly affected by socio-economic status and communication variables to the degree of 78.30 per cent whereas material possession affected confirmation negatively to the confirmation where as overall acceptance of floriculture was significantly affected to the extent 46.60 per cent by innovation proneness, risk orientation and economic motivation.

5

SUMMARY AND CONCLUSION

In olden days, flowers were not of much economic importance. One would grow flowers to fulfil his/her aesthetic sense. With the passage of time, there has been great change in life style of people, leading to commercialization of flowers growing. Today floriculture is recognized as a lucrative business since it has higher potential per unit area than most the field crops even horticultural crops both for domestic market and export (Mishra and Pathania, 2000). The floriculture industry has a bright future as the global floriculture trade is growing at very fast pace in the recent years. The world floriculture market is growing at an annual growth potential of 25 – 30 per cent (Umrao & Singh, 1997).

In the world trade of ornamentals, share of developing countries is only nine per cent, in which India's share is even less than one per cent, in spite of having diverse soil, suitable agroclimatic conditions, large and reputed tissue culture facilities, expert and cheap manpower and developed industrial base. It is because, serious attention was not paid in the past to develop trade on scientific line to exploit its full potentialities.

In recent years, a few large business houses have entered in to floriculture for home consumption as also for export. However, the production and trade of floriculture for traditional and industrial purpose is mainly in hands of small family enterprises, where women folk is prominent worker, the poorer the family, the more it depends on economic productivity of its women. No serious efforts have been done to improve the condition of women in our country. It is only possible through empowerment of women, which can be done through training on floriculture-oriented enterpreneurship. If women would be trained for the job related to floriculture, future prospect of floriculture would be brighter and so will be national development. Considering the importance of floriculture as an income generating activity for farm women, it was felt rational to take the present study with following objectives:

1. To study the existing pattern of flower cultivation technology.
2. To impart technical know how to rural women on flower cultivation.
3. To analyse the acceptability level of flower cultivation enterprise by farm women.

The study was conducted in Sonepat and Panipat districts of Haryana state purposively as these districts have proximity to Delhi and well linked with train and road transport, where there is a national flower market. From these districts, one block from Sonepat i.e Sonepat block and two blocks from Panipat district i.e. Panipat and Matloda blocks were selected randomly. Out of three blocks, 4 villages viz. Jahri and Garh from Sonepat block and Sithana and RamNagar from Panipat and Matloda block respectively selected roundemly. From these villages 2 SHGs formed by Women Awareness and Management Agency per village were selected randomly so as to have a sample of 80 farm women in 8 SHGs.

The independent variables were socio-personal, economic and communication variables of rural women. Acceptability of flower cultivation technology was the dependent variable. Acceptability of the technology was measured in five stages viz; knowledge, persuation, decision, implementation and confirmation as conceptualized by Rogers (1983). With the help of pre-tested interview schedule respondents were assessed for pre knowledge and attitude towards flower cultivation technology. Then five days training on the selected feasible flowers were organised in all the selected villages separately. After training, gain in knowledge, reduction of knowledge gap about various messages of flower cultivation technology, attitude change, mental readiness of the respondents to adopt this technology, cultivation of flowers by the interested respondents on small scale, marketing of flowers, cost-benefit analysis, final adoption of the technology on large scale and finally analysis of factors affecting non-adoption of technology and constraints experienced by the respondents in adoption of flower cultivation as an enterprise were analysed.

A duly pre-tested interview schedule was the tool for data collection. The collected data were then analysed to draw the appropriate inferences by application of suitable statistical tests.

MAIN FINDINGS

The important findings emanated out of the present investigation are as follows:

- Area under floriculture in in Haryana was 2250 ha. Regarding Sonepat and Panipat district flower cultivation was done on 670 and 145 ha respectively. In Jahri village it was 51 ha. and in Garh village it was 63 ha, where as in Sithana and Ram Nagar village there was no area under flower cultivation. Rose and Marigold were main flowers grown during 2001 and 2002.
- Rural women got technical guidance mainly

through DHO, KVK and from progressive farmers. Major source of loaning was banks, DRDA, through credit cards and private financers.

- Sonepat and Panipat local market, connaught place and khari bawli (Delhi) were places mainly visited for marketing of flowers.
- Results of the study revealed that 48.75 per cent respondents belonged to middle age group, low caste (53.75%), having nuclear type family system (72.50%), medium family size (60.00%), land up to 1 acre (53.75%), illiterate (38.75%) and medium income group (40.00%). Farming was the main occupation of all the respondents. More than half of the farm women had medium socio-economic status, low exposure to communication sources (53.75%), high innovation proneness (38.75%), high risk orientation (51.25%) and 60.00 per cent fall under medium economic motivations.
- The knowledge of majority of the respondents at pre-exposure stage regarding flower cultivation was low. Post exposure knowledge level of the trainees indicated that majority were fall under medium and high knowledge level in almost all the message except transplantation, sowing/ planting method and fertilizer application, plant protection and harvesting due to highly technical nature of these messages and illiteracy of the women.
- There was significant difference of knowledge at pre and post exposure stage except fertilizer application.
- The study revealed that there was significant knowledge gap difference in all the messages except harvest and sowing/planting method and fertilizer

application messages.

- Maximum (48.75%) respondents fall under medium knowledge gain index and showed training effectiveness.
- It was observed that 40.00 per cent of the respondents had unfavourable and 60.00 per cent had favourable attitude towards flower cultivation technology at pre-exposure stage whereas at post-exposure stage 96.25 per cent had favourable and only 3.75 per cent had unfavourable attitude.
- More than half of the respondents falls under low attitude change index as they were already convinced about profitability of the floriculture enterprise.
- At post exposure stage, more than half (52.50%) of the respondents made up their mind to adopt the flower cultivation technology for income generation and 41.25 per cent were fully convinced about importance of floriculture. Only five per cent ladies felt very difficulty to procure loan and therefore not ready to implement.
- Situational compatibility followed by cultural compatibility and profitability were major attributes to decide a technology to adopt or reject.
- Adoption feasibility of flower cultivation technology (mean score) was found to be quite high in Garh (4.43) followed by Jahri (4.35), Sithana (4.25) and Ram Nagar (3.20). The overall adoption feasibility village as well as attribute wise was 4.06 (81.20%).
- Adoption feasibility was high of 52.50 per cent respondents followed by medium and low (23.75%) each level.

- It was found that 30.00 per cent respondents put flower cultivation into use immediately after training while 7.50 per cent adopted after some persuation. 40 per cent respondents were interested in adopting whereas, 22.50 per cent farm women were non adopters. In conclusion, it can be said that 77.50 per cent farm women fall under above medium implementation index.
- Highly perishable nature of the crop, marketing problem and non availability or lack of purchasing power were the major reasons for non adoption of the technology.
- Quick deterioration of quality flowers, lack of regular market facilities and difficulty in post harvest management of flowers were the main constraints faced by majority of the farmwomen followed by not able to follow complicated procedure for obtaining loan and non-availability of seed/saplings.
- Gladiolus earn maximum profit of Rs. 70994.80 per acre after a heavy investment of Rs. 88005.20 followed by tuberose which earn Rs. 70159.44 after investment of Rs. 59,840.56 during 2001-2003.
- Total cost of rose cultivation was Rs. 42,611.00 with a net income of Rs. 37,389.00 per acre in a season. After this investment, a continued income can be contained for 4-5 years.
- Unlike gladiolus and tuberose marigold and chrysanthemum require less investment Rs. 19,880.00 and 19,728.24 respectively with a profit of Rs. 12,119.12 and 18,771.76, respectively per acre in a season during 2002-2003.
- It was found that at confirmation stage 86.50 per

cent were the adopters of this technology where as only 12.50 per cent were non adopters.

- The study revealed that 61.25 per cent respondents fall under high confirmation index followed by medium (26.25%) and low (12.50%).
- Overall acceptability tells that 48.75 per cent respondents had medium overall acceptability followed by high (48.75%) and low (16.25%).
- Variables like innovation proneness, risk orientation, economic variables emanated as the main contributory factor to change attitude, decision to adopt, implement, confirm and finally to accept this technology.
- Innovation proneness, risk orientation, economic motivation affected acceptance about flower cultivation to 46.60 per cent variation, where implementation significantly varies to 46.60 per cent with economic motivation. Socio economic status and communication variables significantly affected confirmation to the degree of 78.3 per cent.

RECOMMENDATIONS

Based on the findings of the study following recommendations have been suggested.

1. Sonepat and Panipat are the leading districts in Haryana, has tremendous potential for flower production and both districts have proximity to national capital market of flowers. In spite of having sufficient area under flower cultivation, no planned training are being provided to farm women by any institutions on floriculture, so there is need to train them through self-help groups.

2. Results revealed that the help from District Horticulture Office in the form of bulbs of gladiolus and tuberose, fertiliser and insecticides was available only to same family in same village every year. To bring flower revolution in districts, there is need to approach and motivate different farm women in different village every time.
3. Perceived responses of rural women indicate that there is much need of government support in establishing cold storage facilities, authorised and regularised flower markets, in fixing prices of flowers to check wide fluctuations in sale price. There is also a need to check commission agents in flower market which in turn will help to abolish the 10 per cent ex-orbitant commission from the farm women.
4. Presently, there is a trend of growing roses and marigold flowers but through the present research gladiolus and chrysanthemum have also been found as cost effective crops. So, there is need to popularise these flower crops for commercialisation. In this regard, extension workers at Krishi Vigyan Kendras and District Horticultural Officers can play an important role.
5. Loaning procedures should be simplified so that easy availability of loan on lower rates of interest can be made.
6. Further researches/studies must be conducted to promote floriculture on large scale for better contribution in national development.

SUGGESTED AREAS OF FURTHER RESEARCH

1. Participation of women in floriculture.

2. Marketing pattern of floriculture.
3. Financing pattern of floriculture.
4. Large scale flower production i.e. in green house technology.
5. Training and its impact on floriculture in all villages nearby Delhi and other districts where floriculture enterprise was not practised.
6. Contribution of NGOs and government organisation to promote floriculture and evaluation of involved institution in floriculture.

SELECT BIBLIOGRAPHY

Acharyya, P. and Panda, P.K. (1996). Floriculture- a promising foreign exchange earner. *Yojana* **40(12)**: 17-19

Agarwal, B. (1995). Empower women farmers. *Indian Farmer Times* **15(6)**: 11-12

Ambad, S.N. (1997). Flowers arrangement: an art and beauty. *Ind. Hort* **41(4)**: 4-5

Anita (2000). Acceptability of mushroom production technology by farm women for income generation. MSc. thesis CCS HAU Hisar.

Apte, S.S and Bhargava, S.C. (1998). Indo-Dutch cooperation in floriculture. *Ind. Hort* **43(2)**: 7-13

Arora, J.S. and Singh, K. (2002). Pre and post harvest management of cut flowers. *Ind. Hort* **46(4)**: 20-23

Bala, R. (2000). Farm women participation in selected agricultural and subsidiary occupational activities in Moga district of Punjab. PhD thesis PAU Ludhiana.

Balasudhahari, T. (1997). Post harvest management of cut flowers. *Indian Farmer Times* **14(12)**: 17-18

Behari, O.P. (1993). Marketing of cut-flower in India: An overview. *Agri. Mktg.* **36 (1)**: 6-22

Chattopadhyay, T.K. (2000). Present status of floriculture in West Bengal. *Financing Agriculture* **32 (2)**: 10-15

Chaudhary, M.L. and Prasad, K.V. (2000). Protected cultivation of ornamental crops-an insight. *Ind. Hort* **45 (1)**: 48-53

Chauhan, R.S. (1997). Inside Haryana marigold cultivation is now popular. *Indian Farmer Times* **14(11)**: 19-20

Chhabra, V. (1996). Prospects of floriculture industry in India. *Yojana* **40(12)**: 8-10

Dadlani, N.K. (2002). Promoting floriculture business in India. *Ind. Hort* **46(4)**: 39-43

Dahiya, M. (1999). Adoption of floriculture in Faridabad district of Haryana. MSc. thesis CCS HAU Hisar.

Dahiya, P.; Goyal, S.K. and Pandey, R.N. (1999). Economics analysis of floriculture and competing crops in Sonepat district of Haryana state. *Farmers and Parliament* **36 (6)**: 19-23

Dahiya, P.K. and Goyal, S.K. (2000). Economic feasibility of rose cultivation in Haryana. *Haryana farming* **30 (8)**: 17-18

Das, T.K and Mitra, A. (1994). Some diamentions of marigold (*Targetes erecta* L) marketing in Nadia District of West Bengal-A case study. *Ind. Jour. Agril. Mktg.* **36 (4)**: 24-26

De, L.C. and Dhiman, K.R. (2001). Exploring floriculture potential in Tripura. *Ind. Hort.* **46(3)**: 19-21

Dhawan, V. (2002). Biotechnology in floriculture. *Ind. Hort* **46(4)**: 14-17

Gaikwad, M.R. (1981). Chrysanthemum flower of commercial value. *Farmers and Parliament* **16 (4)**: 18,26-27

Ghosh, S.P. (1999). Horticulture production, marketing and export-the smell of success. *Indian Farming* **49(7)**: 23-28

Gill (2002). Impact of involvement of women in agricultural and allied activities on home environment in Punjab. PhD thesis PAU Ludhiana.

Goyal, S.K. (1999). Economics of rose cultivation and its

marketing in Sonepat district of Haryana state. *Ind. Jour. Agril. Mktg.* **13 (3)**: 44-46

ICAR (2000). Agriculture research data book. Indian Agricultural Statistical Research, ICAR, New Delhi. *pp* 121

Islam; Bhuiyan and Karim (1998). Women participation in agricultural income generating activities. *Rural Dev. Abs.* **21 (1)**: 50

Jadhav, M.S.; Sale, D.L. and Ambad, S. (1997). Domestic and export marketing of selected flowers. *Ind. Jour. Agril. Mktg.* **11 (1&2)**: 42-43

Kadian, R.S.; Karwasra, R.S. and Amrita (1995). Floriculture for higher income. *Haryana Farming* **25(12)**: 25

Kaptan, S.S. (1994). Towards a new dawn. *Social Welfare* **41(6)**: 3-6

Katyayan, B.S. (1989). Flower garden can turn gold mines. *Indian Farmer Times* **6(10)**: 13-14

Khader, V. (1997). Mushroom cultivation for rural women enterpreneurship. *Indian Farming* **19(4)**: 19-25

Kundu, K.K.; Singh, J.; Singh, V.K. and Suhag, K.S. (1997). India's floriculture export-growth, status, constraints and export strategies: an analysis. *Ind. Jour. Agril. Mktg.* **11 (1&2)**: 14-20

Latha, B. and Brindha, N. (1994). Participation of women in seed industry. *Indian Farmer Times* **12(5)**: 17-26

Maity, R.G. (1997). Flowers as a commercial crop in east and north-east. *Yojana* **41(9)**: 21-24

Mehta, S. (1995). Commucation fidelity of need based training for farm women. PhD thesis CCS HAU Hisar.

Mishra, R.L. and Dhankhar, B.S. (2002). Producing flowers in non-conventional areas. *Ind. Hort* **46(4)**: 36-38

Mishra, S. (1994). Invisible workers. *Social Welfare* **41(6)**: 13-14

Misra, A. (1997). Floriculture as a venture of profit. *Indian Farmer Times* **15(1)**: 11-12

Misra, R.L. and Pathania, N.S. (2000). Hi-tech greenhouse and production strategies for cut flowers. *Ind. Hort* **45 (1)**: 8-11,25

N.H.B. (1995). Rastria bagwani board ki suvidhae. *Udhyan Lok.* **7(1)**: 37-38

Negi, J.P. (2002). Role of NHB. *Ind. Hort* **46(4)**: 1-4,26-28

Padmanabhan, B.S. (1991). Unlimited export potential. *The Hindu Survey of Indian Agriculture* (Section5): 197-198

Parameswaran, K. (2002). Flowers Therapy. *Employment News* (9-15 March): 2

Patel, M.R.; Trivedi, J.C.; Desai, C.P. and Patel, A.A. (1996). Participation of rural women in decision making. *Rural Dev. Abs.* **19 (5)**: 250

Pillay, S. (1993). Flowers can make earning easy. *Indian Farmer Times* **11(5)**: 4

Pradhan, M. (1990). Women in agriculture. *Indian Farmers Times* **8 (7)**: 19-20

Qaim, M. (1999). Women in Kenyan agriculture. *Rural Dev. Abs.* **22 (3)**: 201

Raghava, S.P.S. (2001). Floriculture- a viable diversification option in agri-business. *Ind. Hort* **45 (4)**: 41,44-45

Rai, A.N. (1996). Women workers in agriculture. *Indian Farmers Times* **14 (1)**: 22-24

Rai, S.; Rai, A. and Sharma, B.R. (2000). Gladiolus is a subsidiary source of income. *Ind. Hort* **45(11)**: 7-8

Raj, D. (2001). Making floral craft from forest products of the Himalayas. *Ind. Hort* **46(3)**: 26-28

Ramphal (1993). Scope of cut-flower exports from India. *Agri. Mktg.* **36 (1)**: 25-30

Rao, P.S. (2000). Comprehensive floriculture insurance. *Ind. Hort* '**45 (3)**: 4-5

Rao, R. (1994). Women power fuels, India's milk cooperatives. *Social Welfare* **41(6)**: 10-12

Raut, R.C. and Rasane, V.S. (2000). Marketing of roses in Nasik district (Maharashtra). *Ind. Jour. Agril. Mktg.* **14 (2)**: 32-40

Reddy, V. (1996). Horticulture as a commercial venture. *Indian Farmer Times* **14(12)**: 19-21

Saini, G.S. (2001). Growing gladiolus scientifically. *Ind. Hort* **46(2)**: 19-21

Sindhu, S. (1995). Floriculture-boom days ahead. *Indian Farmer Times* **13 (3)**: 15-16

Sandhu, S.S. (1995). Present status of floriculture-challenges, opportunities and constraints. *Farmer and Parliament* **13 (3)**. 15-16

Sangwan, S. (2002). Adoption feasibility of grape products by rural women. MSc. thesis CCS HAU Hisar.

Sebastian, S. (1996). Rose revolution spreading fast. *Indian Farmer Times* **14(2)**: 12-13

Sen, D.and Rani, G.J. (1990). Women in dairing: a case study. *J. of Rural Dev.* **9(5)**: 809-831

Sharma, M.R. (2002). In India: Role of NABARD in promoting floriculture industry with credit support. *Ind. Hort* **46(4)**: 60-63

Sharma, N. (1999). Acceptability of selected drudgery reducing farm implements by farm women: an action research. MSc. thesis CCS HAU Hisar.

Sharma, R.K. (1993). Post harvest handling of flowers-beyond the basics. *Agri. Mktg.* **36 (1)**: 40

Sharma, S. (2003). Development and effectiveness of media on women operated farm machinery for cotton cultivation. PhD thesis CCS HAU Hisar.

Sihag, S. (1995). Participation, knowledge and adoption od dairy innovations among rural women in Haryana. PhD thesis CCS HAU Hisar.

Sindhu, S.S. (1995). Present status of floriculture-challenges, opportunities and constraints. *Farmers and Parliament* **15 (1)**: 21-22

Sindhu, S.S. and Misra, R.L. (1997). Problems and prospects of flowers in India. *Ind. Hort* **42(2)**: 52-53

Singh, A.K.and Bijimal, G. (1999). Growing of gladiolus is lucrative. *Farmers and Parliament* **37 (7)**: 4-6

Singh, B. (1997). Floriculture: an emerging industry in India. *Ind. Hort* **42 (2)**: 47-51

Singh, H.P. (2002). Floriculture industry in India: its perspective. *Ind. Hort* **46(4)**: 51-56

Singh, J.P. (1994). Emerging export opportunities. *The Hindu Survey of Indian Agriculture* (Section4): 129-135

Singh, K. (1997). Export potential of floriculture in Haryana. In course manual: *Agro-technique in horticultural crops.* pp14-24

Singh, M.K., Voleti, S.R. and Sindhu, S.S. (2002). Post harvest handling and care of cut flowers. *Ind. Hort* **46(4)**: 44-45

Srivastava, L.S. (1995). Floriculture in India-retrospect and prospect. *Financing Agri.* **37(3)**: 11-14

Talukdar, R.K. and Karmakar, A. (1999). Problems indecision making by women in agriculture- a study in Golaghat district of Assam. *Rural Dev. Abs.* **22 (1)**: 29

Tomer, B.S. and Singh, K.K. (2001). Producing seed of marigold. *Ind. Hort* **45 (4)**: 36-37

Uberoy, A. (1995). New technologies for women in agriculture. *Yojana* **39(11)**: 17-20

Umrao, V.K. and Singh, A.K. (1997). World trade in floriculture. *Indian Farmers Times* **15 (1)**: 21-22

Vasavada, A.P. (1995). Commercialisation of flower culture. *Indian Farmers Times* **12(11)**: 15-18

Widge, M.K. (1995). Women in agriculture. *Yojana* **39(9)**: 21-23,26

INDEX